Designed For Fulfillment

A Study Of The Redemptive Gifts

By Charles R. Wale, Jr.

Foreword By Arthur Burk

Designed For Fulfillment
A Study Of The Redemptive Gifts

© 2007 Charles R. Wale, Jr.

All rights reserved.

Published by Free To Be Ministries, Inc.
P.O. Box 1340
Amite, LA 70422
www.freetobeministries.com

The foundational concepts and much of this material was originally produced and published by Arthur Burk of Sapphire Leadership Group, 2367 West La Palma Avenue, Anaheim, CA 92801. All materials are used with his permission. You will find a list of resources used on pages 160-61.

Cover Photography by Brent and Tiffany Wale

Cover Design by Jan Gannaway

To contact or order *Designed For Fulfillment*
Free To Be Ministries, Inc.
P. O. Box 1340
Amite, LA 70422

Website: www.freetobeministries.com
Email: chuck@freetobeministries.com
Phone: 601-749-8220

ISBN 1-931379-16-5

Dedication

This book is dedicated to my three granddaughters—
Katelyn, Alanya, and Emma.
They are Papa's blessings from God.

Acknowledgments

I would like to thank my wife Debbie. We have been married thirty years, and I am so blessed to have her in my life. She is a wonderful mother to our three sons (Chip, Brent, and Drew) who are a joy in our lives. Debbie has been a source of encouragement and constructive feedback to me. She may be my wife, but she is also my best friend.

My understanding of redemptive gifts began with an email to Arthur Burk, who introduced me to Nina Lemnah. Thank you, Nina and Arthur, for helping me discover my redemptive gift and putting me on the track of fulfilling my birthright.

Most of the material included in this book comes from the audio teachings of Arthur Burk. This book would not have been possible without Arthur's permission to use his copyrighted materials. Arthur, you truly have blessed me with your generosity and words of wisdom.

Thank you to my son and daughter-in-law for the photography on the cover. It came out beautifully. They have been diligent in carrying the torch of Redemptive Gifts to the next generation. They also provided Debbie and me with the blessing of one of our beautiful granddaughters, Alayna.

I can count on my fingers the number of people that I consider best friends. One of those is Sylvia Gunter. She has become like a sister and a dear friend to me. She has patiently worked with me to produce this book. Those who know me know I need to process out loud much of the time. She has provided a listening ear and thoughtful feedback for my off-the-wall ideas and comments until the seeds of my thoughts bore fruit.

I want to thank Elizabeth Gunter Wallace for a beautiful job of designing and editing the original manuscript. Elizabeth took the initial ore and turned it into a precious gem. Her ideas encouraged me to produce something that was much better than I ever imagined. She also provided youthful energy that I lacked. Everyone who knows her knows what a blessing she is.

Bernie and Randy Howard, Geoff Morris, and Neil Barberio were kind enough to read the original manuscript and provide editing comments and constructive criticism. Thank you for the hours you invested and invaluable input you made.

To my Father in Heaven, thank you for blessing me with such wonderful people in my life who have brought out the best in me. Without the divine appointments orchestrated by you, none of us would have crossed paths, and I would have been the worse off for it. You knew exactly who and what I needed to fulfill my destiny and birthright.

3

Have you ever attempted to assemble a 1,000 piece picture puzzle without looking at the picture on the lid of the box? No fun!

If you have been bumping against people all through your life when you really wanted to connect with them, you might be working without seeing the master plan. Once you see the big picture, it is easier to find out how you connect properly with the other people around you.

If you will study this manual, it WILL help you form community more easily, with far more gratifying results.

Where did you have your best experience of being "in community?" Your high school football team when you were a letterman? The first few years of your marriage? The worship team at church? The people in the office who support your work in the field?

It really doesn't matter what YOUR answer is because whichever one you answered "yes" to, brought painful memories to at least ten other people reading the list.

Why? One of the major reasons is because we do not know how we are made and how we are supposed to fit together with others.

In this book, Chuck explores many different angles of the redemptive gifts of individuals. These gifts are your "hard-wiring" from God. When you understand what you bring to a relationship and what you need from a relationship, it is easier to form mutually life-giving relationships.

Life is not a cakewalk, and this book is not pabulum. I encourage you to dedicate hundreds of hours over the next few years to studying the concepts laid out here. These treasures will need to be absorbed slowly and deeply into your life. They can't just be put on like a tee shirt.

If you will dig in, it could bring you a far greater return on investment than just about any other growth project you have invested in.

So go for it. Community is essential, so you may as well learn to do it with excellence and joy.

Arthur Burk
Anaheim, CA
Sept. 2007

5

In the beginning God created...
Genesis 1:1

Before we came into being, God had a plan for us. Psalm 139 says that we are fearfully and wonderfully made by our Creator who created our innermost being in our mother's womb. God chose our physical appearance as well as our innermost parts. He is a master craftsman who works with absolute intensity and intentionality. Each of us is a reflection of him, created in his image for his good pleasure. ***Designed For Fulfillment*** is an attempt to take a closer look at a part of that plan in order to better understand ourselves and our design.

My first introduction to the concept of spiritual gifts came from a Basic Institutes Seminar led by Bill Gothard many years ago. Bill Gothard differentiates between the gifts of the Spirit mentioned in Romans 12, 1 Corinthians 12, and Ephesians 4. He referred to the gifts of the Spirit listed in Romans 12 as "motivational gifts," the gifts in 1 Corinthians as "manifestational gifts," and the gifts mentioned in Ephesians as "offices." Years later, my understanding of the spiritual gifts was greatly expanded through the teaching of Arthur Burk. He has done an enormous amount of study on the seven gifts in Romans 12. He refers to this list of gifts as the seven "redemptive gifts," and that is the language adopted in this book.

Identifying your gifting is merely a starting point. There is so much more to the redemptive gifts than just obtaining a label. I'm a Giver. That's nice. So what? How does that change and affect the way I interact with God, myself, and others? A redemptive gift is also more than a personality profile. Understanding the redemptive gifts will give you a greater understanding of the potential that you have, as well as the difficulties that you face. It will help you identify your individual strengths and weaknesses. You will begin to understand in a deeper way why God created you. You will learn to stop wasting your time on those things that are motivated by woundedness rather than by your Father's design. Your love of your Father will go to a deeper level as you begin to see more clearly his love and destiny for you. In short, you will recognize in a new way what it means to be a child of the Most High God.

This manual is an attempt to answer the "so what" question. Arthur Burk, Nina Lemnah, Sylvia Gunter, and others helped me develop the skeleton of understanding I have concerning the redemptive gifts. They were instrumental in helping me to identify my redemptive gift. They also helped me to answer the "so what" question for my own life. ***Designed For Fulfillment*** is intended for you to learn about and then teach the subject of redemptive gifts. It includes a discussion of the characteristics of each redemptive gift and incorporates information on curses, blessings, and scale of responsibility for each gift on a number line from –100 to +100. It includes a brief discussion of the sevens in Scripture and redemptive gifts of cities, states, and countries. Much of this material has been gleaned from the teachings of Arthur Burk, and he has graciously consented to the use of his material. Many others have also contributed their observations and conclusions. We have attempted to extract and compile details from all these sources so that you have at your fingertips a more complete picture of redemptive gifts.   Chuck Wale

Designed For Fulfillment — What Does It Mean?

*"I have come that you might have life, and have it **to the full**"*
John 10:10 NIV

Have you set out to fulfill the dreams and aspirations that you know God has given you, only to find them delegitimized by others? Instead of walking in God's freedom to be who he designed you to be, you find yourself chasing after something that, though good on the surface, is designed to fulfill someone else.

The literal meaning of the phrase "Designed For Fulfillment" is to conceive or execute a plan that develops the full potentialities. Yet this definition falls short of adequately expressing the full meaning that needs to be conveyed.

It is my belief that God has uniquely designed each of us to fulfill the dream or vision that is uniquely accomplished by our redemptive gift. In other words, the road to fulfillment starts by understanding God's redemptive design for us and allowing it to guide our footsteps.

Fulfillment comes when we use all the abilities that God gave us and know that we know that we are doing exactly what our Father designed for us. Fulfillment comes when we are walking in our unique design and fully developing the resources that God has placed within us. To the degree that we understand our design and use our calling and talents according to this design, we will live fulfilled.

You are free to be who God made you to be. When you come into alignment with who God designed you to be and achieve your calling, you will be enormously fulfilled, and the world will be blessed.

Chuck Wale

Personal Testimonies

The discovery of the redemptive gifts has changed my life. When I found out I was not a teacher but an exhorter, an important puzzle piece dropped into place. I now have a foundation and words to express who I am and what I was born to do. I chose my new business career based on being an exhorter, and I have been fairly successful. At the same time, it has opened wide issues with my spirit, soul, and character that are tough to look at and require time to deal with and practice. This is not an instant, drive-through, overnight, three-simple-steps-to-completeness, just-add-water-and-mix formula. Although the principles are simple, it is not easy. But then again, anything worth obtaining never is. There is hope in exploring these parts of the kingdom, because Abba has placed in each of us a unique design through our awesome identity to give life to the body of Christ. — **Drew Richards, insurance businessman/exhorter**

Grasping how God has designed the redemptive gifts has really been a blessing to us and our ministry. When we first stumbled upon the redemptive gifts, we honestly felt a little overwhelmed. It was like trying to drink from a fire hydrant. The information in this manual is presented in a manner that helped us to see the big picture and allowed us to see the details and their application in our lives. It provided us with the tools we needed to minister to others. Thank you from the bottom of our hearts. — **Brent and Tiffany Wale, youth ministers/exhorter and teacher**

Hearing this teaching made me accept and even appreciate myself the way God made me. Before, I always felt like he was expecting me to try to be like others, especially those with giftings that include the "stronger" or more forceful personalities. I can rest more easily in my own skin now and am much more comfortable in social situations. I can be myself more easily and not so much of a chameleon, trying to be everything to everyone. My husband is teacher redemptive gift. The way he has to research and analyze everything before making a decision used to drive me crazy. Now I accept and even embrace it as part of the territory in being a teacher. In general, I can look at people now and figure out what their gift is, maybe not exactly, but close enough to understand why they act as they do. That makes it a lot easier to work with different types of people, especially in the workplace. — **Bernie Howard, technical assistant/mercy**

Knowledge of redemptive gifts has helped me in all my relationships, but it has most affected my relationship with my sister. I have always loved my sister, but she seemed to be the only person who could push my buttons. She is a prophet gift, and I am a ruler, which seems to cause each of us to interpret the processing of words differently. Now when we seem to be stepping into a conflict, she will say, "This is what I said, but you understood it to be this, and that is not what I meant." We now know how each other processes information, and we understand each other better. The redemptive gifts have been a blessing to all of us!

— **Susie Adams, secretary/ruler**

As a servant, I lived as a victim all my life until learning about redemptive gifts and applying it. I have learned that I have authority. I have chosen to live in dominion, and I thank God that now I see positive changes. I have also learned that I have authority over death and physical spirits, and God is showing me how to apply this. Studying redemptive gifts has taught me how to understand other people so that I can relate to the other gifts in the way that God desires.

— **Elizabeth Cupstid, contracts manager/servant**

The benefit for me of discovering my redemptive gift was to identify the growth areas that would yield the greatest results for the effort. To recognize and commit my inherent weaknesses to the cross, "to embrace the pain" of my sanctification, has opened up opportunities to experience and offer more of the grace of God! — **Emory Putman, pastor/teacher**

Because of the redemptive gift teaching we found ourselves, for the first time ever, reconciled to ourselves and to each other. We were two people who loved one another, yet we seemed to be at war with each other because of the diversity of our redemptive gifts (prophet and teacher). This teaching helped us understand that we can choose to be as life-giving to ourselves, each other, and others as we had been destructive in times past. We continue to grow and become as we incorporate this understanding for ourselves and for others. We look forward to each day as our spirits grow larger and our skillset increases, so we can be better problem-solvers and see others grow large in their spirit.— **Larry and Ann Patrick, prophet and teacher**

When I was in Bible school eight years ago, I took a class on the gifts, and at that time I felt that everyone in the kingdom of God needs to understand this important teaching. This advanced teaching has blessed me so much. I have had many opportunities to speak into the lives of people, especially those who are servant or mercy gift, encouraging them to come into a fuller understanding of their call. I desire to enhance the lives of others and help encourage all to come into a fuller aspect of who they are in Christ through teaching the gifts. — **Cynthia I. Celli, giver**

As I began to embrace the redemptive gift teaching, it has broadened my perspective of the role of diversity in the body of Christ. It has helped me understand how God has purposefully designed His people to reflect His redemptive gifts, with each person having a unique and creative way of expressing the sevenfold character of God. Instead of thinking of unity in terms of conformity, seeing the different ways God designed each redemptive gift to fit together as a diverse, organic whole has given me a greater appreciation of the uniqueness of others. An analogy that comes to mind is that of a work of fine art. The master painter dips his brush into a variegated palette of colors, but uses them in a way that a beautiful painting emerges from the depths of his creativity. When the painting is displayed, the entire world can see that its colorful beauty reflects the creative impulse of the artist. Learning my own primary "coloring" (gifting) has enhanced my willingness to let God mix my color with the other colors he has on His palate (the body of Christ) as God paints His masterpiece on the canvas of human history.

— **Geoff Morris, communications technician/mercy**

My first response to the redemptive gifts was "I don't want to be pigeon-holed." Then as God began to reveal who I was in specific gifts, I began to identify and receive them as part of myself as a whole. As each part of my spirit began to awaken to my specific gift, it changed how I saw God, myself, and the people around me. For example, my son was going through a difficult situation. He asked me questions pertaining to "What now?" "Why do I react this way?" etc. As I tried to understand him, I gave him descriptions of two redemptive gifts to read. I could hear him in the other room. First a "What?" Then a "Hmmm." Then an out-and-out laugh. He came into the room where I was and declared, "I thought I was weird, but this so totally described me. Mom, this is me!" I have watched him over the years struggle with finding his place and with trying to be something he wasn't but not really understanding who he was. I cannot express the joy in listening and watching him respond to a description of his redemptive gift and identifying with who God made him to be. Incredible! Now my response is, what an incredible tool to be applied, whether it is in my personal relationship with my Father or my relationship with my husband, my child, or community (church or work). — **Debbie Sample, ministry assistant/servant**

I was utterly stunned by Chuck's teaching on redemptive gifts. I came skeptical and left a believer! Not only did the teaching explain to me who I was, it explained to me the different people that I have worked with and the reason for the problems I had encountered. This is good stuff! — **Jim Long, pastor/teacher**

Table Of Contents

Who Am I Really?

If you ever walked the halls of a fine art museum, you may have noticed that every great piece of art is surrounded by a magnificent frame. A canvas is incomplete without its frame. Each of us is a canvas of God's creation. He has painted each of us in a unique set of colors and brush stokes. While the canvas of who we are may be radically different from those around us, there are four basic truths that are universal. These four truths serve as the frame of each canvas. So as we begin our study of redemptive gifts, all of what is shared should be seen in the frame of the following foundational truths.

1. You are uniquely you. You are special.

Psalm 139:13-16 says, "For you created my inmost being; you knit me together in my mother's womb. I praise you because I am fearfully and wonderfully made; your works are wonderful, I know that full well. My frame was not hidden from you when I was made in the secret place. When I was woven together in the depths of the earth, your eyes saw my unformed body. All the days ordained for me were written in your book before one of them came to be." When you were formed in your mother's womb, you were formed by God's love and passion and intentional design. God brought you forth with unique qualities that would please him, be fulfilling to you, and be desperately needed by others. God has given each person a unique "spiritual DNA," so that you can be who he wants you to be and allow him to do what he wants to do through you.

2. You are uniquely you for a purpose. Nobody can take your place in your world.

Ephesians 2:10 says "For we are God's workmanship, created in Christ Jesus to do good works, which God prepared in advance for us to do." God uniquely made you to be the person you are for his good purposes. You are designed to be a part of his bigger story. God imparts to you and equips you with spiritual gifts for his purposes and plans.

3. You are uniquely crafted and placed in this time in history and in this certain place.

Acts 17:26 says, "God determined the times set for them and the exact places where they should live." Esther was told, "Who knows but that you have come to royal position for such a time as this?" (Esther 4:14). God has placed you in your place for such a time as this. You have a strategic position in a strategic place in a strategic time.

4. You are uniquely gifted and needed by those God has called you to be with.

Peter said, "Each one should use whatever gift he has received to serve others, faithfully administering God's grace in its various forms. If anyone speaks, he should do it as one speaking the very words of God. If anyone serves, he should do it with the strength God provides, so that in all things God may be praised through Jesus Christ" (1 Peter 4:10-11). Your God-given gifting is needed by your family and community of faith. Romans 12:4-5 says, "Just as each of us has one body with many members, and these members do not all have the same function, so in Christ we who are many form one body, and each member belongs to all the others." One may be a hand, another may be a foot, someone else is the eye, but when they all are functioning, the body can walk about and do what it is supposed to do (1 Corinthians 12:12-25).

13

What Is The Biblical Foundation For Redemptive Gifts?

The Bible lists spiritual gifts in Romans 12, 1 Corinthians 12, and Ephesians 4. These lists are based on different Greek words for gift used in 1 Corinthians 12:4-7. "There are different kinds of gifts (charisma), but the same Spirit. There are different kinds of service (diakonia), but the same Lord. There are different kinds of working (energema), but the same God works all of them in all men. Now to each one the manifestation (phanerosis) of the Spirit is given for the common good." Each of these Scriptures is unique in their wording and meaning, revealing a distinct and different purpose for each list of gifts. The true beauty of God's design is revealed when we understand the distinctive roles and how they compliment one another perfectly.

Romans 12:6-8

We have different gifts, according to the grace given us. If a man's gift is prophesying, let him use it in proportion to his faith. If it is serving, let him serve; if it is teaching, let him teach; if it is encouraging, let him encourage; if it is contributing to the needs of others, let him give generously; if it is leadership, let him govern diligently; if it is showing mercy, let him do it cheerfully.

The list of gifts in Romans 12:6-8 seems to be foundational. The Greek word for gift in Romans 12 is *charisma*, indicating a gift of grace that is a basic inward drive or bent. These are referred to as the motivational gifts or redemptive gifts. In this book the gifts will be called prophet, servant, teacher, exhorter, giver, ruler, and mercy. All of us have different measures or portions of each of the seven gifts operative in our lives. Usually one of the gifts represents our basic inward drive and is the dominant gift. The seven gifts in Romans 12 shape our views on life circumstances, others, ourselves, and God. It is the mindset that God gives us through which we interpret life and respond, make decisions, choose ministry, enjoy friends, choose a mate, etc. Our dominant gift causes us to see life through a particular point of view with certain spiritual assumptions.

I Corinthians 12:7-11

Now to each one the manifestation of the Spirit is given for the common good. To one there is given through the Spirit the message of wisdom, to another the message of knowledge by means of the same Spirit, to another faith by the same Spirit, to another gifts of healing by that one Spirit, to another miraculous powers, to another prophecy, to another distinguishing between spirits, to another speaking in different kinds of tongues, and to still another the interpretation of tongues. All these are the work of one and the same Spirit, and he gives them to each one, just as he determines.

The second list of gifts may be called manifestation gifts. They are the result of the work or impartation of the Holy Spirit. These nine manifestation or ministry gifts are word of wisdom, word of knowledge, faith, gifts of healing, miraculous powers, prophecy, distinguishing of spirits, speaking in different kinds of tongues, and interpretation of tongues. A believer may have any number of these gifts operational at any particular time. There is a very clear command in

14

1 Corinthians that believers are to seek specific gifts. This implies that as believers beginning their life in Christ, they do not have all the manifestation gifts that God wants to give them. He gives permission to ask for other gifts, although there is no guarantee that God will give everything that is asked for. They are, after all, gifts. So the timing of receiving manifestation gifts and the number of gifts a person has is determined by God.

Ephesians 4:11-13

It was he who gave some to be apostles, some to be prophets, some to be evangelists, and some to be pastors and teachers, to prepare God's people for works of service, so that the body of Christ may be built up until we all reach unity in the faith and in the knowledge of the Son of God and become mature, attaining to the whole measure of the fullness of Christ.

The third list in Ephesians 4:11-12 is a list of "offices" or "governmental gifts" for the benefit of the maturity of the church. Paul is describing the roles established by God to serve and build up the body of Christ until they become mature, attaining to the whole measure of the fullness of Christ. These five offices are pastor, prophet, teacher, evangelist, and apostle. Throughout history, godly believers have been raised up to serve the body of Christ in these various roles.

Good and godly people disagree about which of these lists of gifts are still active in the church today. For the purposes of this study, we will hold to the biblical idea that everybody has one of the seven redemptive gifts outlined in Romans 12 that most defines their spiritual identity. It has been my experience that one of the seven gifts from Romans 12 is typically most defining of an individual's overall character. God perfectly reflects all seven of the gifts; and, since mankind is created in his image, God intends that everyone should reflect these seven redemptive gifts in various levels. As people live their Christian life on the foundation of their redemptive gift, they can receive and minister with any combination of the manifestation gifts from 1 Corinthians 12. There will be some who also operate in one of the governmental gifts listed in Ephesians 4. For example, a person with the redemptive gift of mercy may operate in some of the gifts listed in 1 Corinthians 12, as well as serve in an office or governmental gift listed in Ephesians 4, such as pastor. One example from Scripture is John, who held the office of apostle (Ephesians 4), had the redemptive gift of mercy (Romans 12), and wrote the prophetic book of Revelation (1 Corinthians 12). John is a beautiful representation of how these three distinct lists of gifts complement one another instead of contradicting each other.

The purpose of this book is not to debate or persuade another's theological views. I desire to bring more clarity and awareness to the whole body of Christ about our unique design. Ultimately, I desire for this study to awaken in you a deeper intimacy with your Father as you understand the way he designed you. I also want it to be the means for you to celebrate the uniqueness of the glory of God expressed in others in your life, family, community of faith, and the world.

Why Study The Redemptive Gifts?

To Understand Your Design

Many people who have journeyed through this study on redemptive gifts have had common responses. "I'm normal, I'm normal!" "Why didn't someone tell me this before?" "Wow, that explains a lot." For most people, the knowledge of how God designed them is liberating. We all grow up in families, schools, churches, communities, and nations that attempt to mold and shape us into what they think is acceptable for us. Sometimes their picture and God's picture is the same, and the person feels affirmed and accepted. Often other people's definition of "normal" is far from what God designed in us. Learning about the characteristics of the redemptive gifts gives us the freedom to be who God has designed us to be.

Understanding your design allows you to live in your birthright. Your birthright goes hand-in-hand with your redemptive gift. Your birthright is that sense of "This is who I am. This is who God made me. This is what God made me for. I was born for this, and I am accomplishing what God called me to do." It is a tragedy for a person to lack understanding of who they are, what their birthright is, or what they have to do to possess it. It should be normal for people to know what their redemptive gift is and to live from their birthright with a profound sense of fulfillment.

To Benefit The Body Of Christ

God gave the gifts to benefit the body of Christ. According to Ephesians 2:22, we are being built together to be a habitation of God in the Spirit. As we live and minister from our giftedness, we take our place in God's corporate plans and purposes. Understanding the strengths and weaknesses of each of the redemptive gifts, and how they relate to each other, helps people serve in a way that can most effectively benefit the body of Christ.

- For example, the gift of servant is designed by God to be very flexible, to make quick adjustments, to fix anything that needs to be fixed. This is a perfect fit for children's ministry. On the other hand, the gift of teacher is a planner who likes things to be in order. The teacher gift is not nearly as adaptable to change and flexible as the servant gift. Thus, you probably wouldn't want the teacher gift primarily working in the always-changing, never-predictable world of 3-year-olds.

- With the gift of giving, people generally think of money, but it is far more creative a gift than mere financial stewardship, especially when this gift joins together with one of the other gifts. For example, the gift of prophet can conceive an idea, but the giver has the special gift for birthing and nurturing the new concepts and ideas conceived by the prophet. When the prophet and giver work together to bring forth something new, it is a powerful combination. Understanding the gifts and how they relate to each other helps benefit the faith community as it is being "fitly framed together" (Ephesians 2:21).

A leader must learn how to utilize the gifted people that God brings together to effectively benefit the body of Christ. Imagine a room with the world's best athlete, finest musician, greatest artist, most accurate theologian, greatest statesman, and most brilliant scientist. It is an impressive collection of gifted talent, but it does no good when what is needed at the time is a brain surgeon. Though talented, a musician cannot do the job of a surgeon because they are not gifted in that particular area. In a similar way, each redemptive gift has certain strengths and abilities by God's design. A servant is not designed to do the job of a ruler, and neither is the mercy gift primarily designed to do the job of an exhorter because they are foundationally different. Learning the strengths and weaknesses of each redemptive gift helps us to understand the ways God has designed his people to flow and function together as "one body." The apostle Paul stated it this way when describing how the faith community matured into Christ: "From him the whole body, joined and held together by every supporting ligament, grows and builds itself up in love, as each part does its work" (Ephesians 4:16).

To Improve Relationships

Not only does the faith community benefit from understanding the redemptive gifts, a marriage also profits from understanding the gifts. When two people marry, they bring their own distinct gifts to the marriage. When a couple understands the seven redemptive gifts, they can adapt to situations by letting their gifts complement each other, instead of expecting their partner to think and be like them. For example, prophets can change their mind very quickly when God speaks a new direction to them. On the other hand, the mercy gift takes longer to process things emotionally. When a prophet husband and a mercy wife come together in marriage, the husband does well to recognize that his wife may need time to process new ideas and new directions. If a prophet husband does not understand this aspect of the mercy gift, he may think his wife lacks faith or is in rebellion to what God is saying. However, it is not wrong for the mercy person to process change more slowly, because it is the way God designed the mercy gift. It is one way God sets up checks and balances in the marriage. Neither is it wrong for the prophet to change directions quickly. The prophet's decisiveness can help the mercy to more forward with a new direction. At the same time, God designed the mercy to hold the impulsive prophet in balance, because the prophet tends to chase after new things too quickly. By understanding the redemptive gifts, it allows for more grace in a marriage, as husband and wife partner with each other with better understanding and more harmony by allowing their strengths and weaknesses to complement each other.

Understanding redemptive gifts is also beneficial in the parenting of natural and spiritual children. Since each gift has natural strengths and weakness, each particular gift has specific challenges in parenting. For example, the servant desires to meet needs, especially when it comes to their children, because it is a part of their spiritual birthright. However, the servant will often serve their children in excessive ways, causing them to have unrealistic expectations about how much employers, friends, and others around them will meet their needs. When the servant understands that their calling is to empower and release instead of enabling, they can refocus

17

their energies and minimize their weaknesses. Helping both parents and children understand their redemptive gifts can bring a deeper love and appreciation for one another. Another example is a child with the redemptive gift of prophet who grew up with a parent with the redemptive gift of teacher. The redemptive gift of prophet knows no fear and desires to be on the cutting edge of things. The teacher, however, is slow to warm up to new ideas and likes the safety of established methods. Because the prophet did not learn about the characteristics of their particular gift until much later in life, he may have felt the pain of rejection from the teacher parent while growing up because of the teacher's tendency to be slow in receiving new ideas. But by learning the character traits of the redemptive gifts, the prophet can better understand that their teacher parent was not rejecting them personally, but rather may have unintentionally caused them pain because of their natural tendencies. The Bereans readily received Paul and Silas into the synagogue of the Jews, but needed time to search out the "new" message of the Gospel in the Hebrew Scriptures before they accepted it to be truth (Acts 17:10-11). So too the teacher does not typically receive the prophet's "new" ideas without processing it over time. By learning about the divergent character traits of the redemptive gifts, such as our example of the prophet child and teacher parent, we can learn to appreciate the differences that God has uniquely designed in each other, allowing reconciliation and healing of past wounds from our upbringing, as well as helping us to parent our natural and spiritual children in ways that give them the freedom to experience life from the perspectives unique to their particular redemptive gift.

Understanding the redemptive gifts is beneficial to all types of relationships. In the workplace, an employer or team leader should consider the individual gifts of their team to determine the best possible position for each person and what motivates each individual to perform their best. For example, suppose you are an employer with a manager whose redemptive gift is ruler. A ruler will not need a lot of relational time from their leader. Just give them a goal and let them go for it. However, if the manager has the redemptive gift of servant, he will need relational care on a more regular basis. He will need to feel that he is meeting a need and playing a vital role in the whole scheme of things in order to stay motivated and feel that he is part of the team.

A Word Of Caution

Redemptive gifts are not to be used as an excuse. Jesus was all seven of the gifts, and the more we mature, the more we look like him in all areas. The redemptive gifts should never be used as an excuse for not ministering or not growing in particular areas. The gift of prophet has a great capacity for faith. Other people have to work at it. The mercy has a great capacity for compassion and doesn't have to work at it. It is wrong for the gift of prophet to say, "Compassion isn't my thing because I'm a prophet." All believers are called to live the fruit of the Spirit and the character of Christ. Everyone is responsible to work diligently on each character quality of Jesus, even those that don't come easily. Everyone is called to have a servant's heart, to show mercy, to give, etc. This is a matter of obedience, regardless of their gifting. This redemptive gift study is a tool for deeper understanding, but in no way should it be used as an excuse for selective growth or disobedience to the clear commands of Scripture.

How Do You Discover Your Dominant Gift?

Suppose you have a bag of small animals. You reach into this bag and grab something, and pull it out. You look at it and say, "It has two wings, white feathers, orange beak, orange webbed feet, lays eggs, swims really well, waddles when it walks, and quacks. In all probability this is a duck." You based that on external characteristics. You didn't need to cut the duck open to see what's inside to determine that. In a similar way, we can observe external behavioral characteristics of the seven gifts. We can observe whether someone is quiet or verbally expressive, whether someone has an independent spirit and prefers to work alone or prefers to be in a group, whether someone is task-oriented or relational-oriented. These things say something about a person and their gift. This section contains a list of general characteristics for each of the seven gifts and a biblical example of each gift. Most people will easily resonate with one gift more than the others. As you read the profiles of the redemptive gifts, consider the following questions.

 ## What motivates your heart?

God gave you a life-long heart motive or redemptive gift. Satan may have spent all of your life denying you the truth of this gift. Take time to examine your life experience to see what God has been revealing to you all along about your design.

What gift seems to fit your natural tendencies?

Where do you come alive? What leaves you feeling drained? Without knowing anything about redemptive gifts, most can come up with a list of answers to those questions. There are tasks that we may be capable of doing, but it does not spur us on to want to do more. For a gift of prophet, the repetitive, strictly structured, methodical nature of being an accountant would be exhausting. For a servant, serving as the spokesperson, in the spotlight, would be uncomfortable.

How do you respond to weaknesses in others?

Each gift views people and circumstances from the mindset of their own gift. When others don't see things as you see them, you may get upset. Do you find yourself taking up for the underdog and being irritated with those who are unkind to them? Are you irritated with a prophet or exhorter who is not picking up on another person's emotional pain? You may be a mercy.

What do your close friends and family see in you?

Show the list of characteristics to a few people who know you well and are trustworthy. What do they say that they see in you?

Most important, what does your heavenly Father have to say?

He is the one who designed you. Ask him to reveal and affirm his design of you.

Read the following descriptions of the seven redemptive gifts and place a check in the box next to each characteristic that strongly describes you. After you have read all seven descriptions, you should have one profile that you identify with most. This is most likely your dominant redemptive gift.

21

Prophet

- ☐ Tends to see things in black and white, right and wrong.

- ☐ Is committed to truth. If it is right and God has said it, the prophet is committed to go regardless of whether anybody follows.

- ☐ Takes initiative and enjoys things that are new. Does a terrible job of maintaining things.

- ☐ Is verbally expressive and can be compulsive about it.

- ☐ Processes quickly. Has an opinion on everything and is quick to share it.

- ☐ Judges and evaluates everything, even situations that do not directly impact him.

- ☐ Knows no fear. Has a basic boldness. Not intimidated by the unknown or change.

- ☐ Needs to have a goal, a reason to live, an objective.

- ☐ Cannot tolerate having no options.

- ☐ Is generous but can give impulsively and unwisely at times.

- ☐ Shifts gears quickly from one direction to another. Can be here and then there.

- ☐ Tends to be a visionary.

- ☐ Is fiercely independent and competitive.

- ☐ Requires full disclosure of facts. Has a compulsion for honesty, integrity, and transparency.

- ☐ Is intolerant of perceived rebellion, hypocrisy, and denial, especially in leadership.

- ☐ Is hard on himself. Tends to find it difficult to forgive himself.

- ☐ Has to make sense out of everything, even unreasonable situations.

- ☐ Can be unsentimental about relationships.

- ☐ Has a passion for excellence in himself and others. Is driven to excel and challenge others to be their best.

- ☐ Has a large range of emotions. Has intense, passionate extremes in emotions.

- ☐ Bases faith on the principles of God's Word. "God said it. I believe it."

- ☐ Can embrace a problem and figure out how to repair it. Can re-build, not just criticize.

- ☐ Needs times alone to refuel and re-energize and process.

- ☐ Has a passion for restoration. Sees the damage of sin and the restoring power of God.

22

- Is drawn to brokenness and can rebuild a broken life.

- Is quick to celebrate what God has done. Has a passion for celebration.

- God often calls the prophet to a higher level of sacrifice in his personal disciplines, faith, and commitment.

- Can go through seasons when God is silent. These seasons of silence are designed to build a deeper root system of faith for greater fruit in the future.

Major Weaknesses

- Judgmental. Critical toward others and even more critical of themselves.

- Unforgiving. Not willing to overlook the failures and weaknesses of others.

- Bitterness. The enduring battlefield for the prophet. Can have an unforgiving spirit that is destructive.

- Non-relational. Tends to value principles and truth as more important than relationships.

Important note: The redemptive gift of prophet does not necessarily have the manifestation gift of prophesy listed in I Corinthians 12 or the office of prophet in Ephesians 4.

Biblical Example Of Prophet — Peter

Peter demonstrated zeal, passion, impulsiveness, and verbal expressiveness. He was the first one to speak in a group more often than anybody else and was a spokesman for the early church (Matt 15:15; 16:16; 17:4; 19:27; John 6:38; 13:6; Acts 2:14; 3:12; 4:8; 11:4). Prophets are intolerant of rebellion and hypocrisy, especially in leadership. Peter confronted Ananias and Sapphira in the early church (Acts 5:1-12). The prophet desires justice, which can lead to unforgiveness. Peter asked how many times he had to forgive those who sinned against him (Matt 18:21). The prophet is hard on himself when he fails. Peter publicly confessed his sinfulness (Luke 5:8). He wept bitterly after he denied Jesus (Luke 22:62).

The prophet makes a quick response to truth or revelation. The prophet has a basic boldness when facing the unknown. Peter asked Jesus to bid him come to him walking on the water (Matt 14:28). For the prophet, truth can be more important than relationships. Peter's motivation for staying with Jesus was that he had the truth; he would stay even if others left him (John 6:67-69). The prophet is articulate in defining right and wrong, black and white. On Pentecost Peter preached that the Jews had crucified Jesus (Acts 2:23). The prophet tends to correct others who are not their business to correct. Peter rebuked Jesus for telling the disciples that he was going to die (Mark 8:31-32). The prophet tends to have to go through more difficulty than others. Peter was willing to suffer shame for the truth of the gospel (Acts 5:29-42).

Servant

- Sees external needs of comfort and food and is quick to meet those needs.

- Is a team player. Is relatively free from the desire to build his own kingdom.

- Is very practical. Is committed to the present moment to meet present needs.

- Has difficulty saying "no" to competing demands. Usually overcommitted in scheduling.

- Finds it hard to accept excellence in his work, to affirm himself, or to receive affirmation from others. Tends to find something to apologize for when serving others.

- Has few enemies.

- Sees the best in others.

- Has high loyalty to family.

- Is not easily angered except when someone hurts a friend or family member.

- Tends to save stuff, but not in a particularly organized manner.

- Is totally trustworthy and reliable.

- Works very hard, often to the harm of their physical health.

- Can make excuses to justify others' bad behavior. Can become enablers, especially to immature people. Wise servants learn to empower, not to enable others.

- Tends to spoil children, meeting too many needs too often. An immature servant may be in denial regarding their children's shortcomings.

- Attracts dishonor, especially in the home. Tends to be the one who is talked down to and has jokes made about them. A servant seems to allow this to happen.

- Is competitive in areas that are considered safe to the servant, such as games or children's sports teams. Otherwise dedicated to seeing others succeed more than himself.

- Has purity of motive. Is straight-forward, honest and can be trusted.

- Prefers not to be visible. Does not desire the spotlight.

- Can be in a sinful environment without getting personally defiled (example: Esther).

- Tends to be exploited by others. Tends to have a victim mentality.

- Responds well to truth.

- Can struggle with issues of shame. May believe they deserve to be the victim.

❏ Wrestles with self-worth. Tends to believe that "I'm not worthy. Others are more worthy."

❏ Desires to empower others to achieve their best. Greatest fulfillment comes in knowing he enables somebody else to do their work. Is drawn to pray for leadership and make them successful.

Major Weaknesses

❏ Battle for self-worth. Doesn't see his innate value and doesn't believe God's truth about himself or his call.

❏ Worry/anxiety. Takes on other people's problems and worries about the problem.

❏ Enabling. Does a task instead of teaching others to do it and releasing it to them.

Biblical Example Of Servant — Esther

We see the redemptive gift of servant in Esther. Servants work well with others and live relatively free from the desire to build their own kingdom. Consequently, they have few enemies and may enjoy a high level of favor. When it came time for Esther to go before the king the first time, Scripture says that "she requested nothing … and Esther obtained favor in the sight of all who saw her" (Esther 2:15). Most people, when elevated to a position such as Esther, would have the tendency to be very demanding of their subordinates. Not Esther. She "requested nothing" and gained favor in the sight of all who saw her.

Servants see the external needs of comfort and are quick to meet those needs. When Esther heard that Mordecai was in sackcloth, her first response was not to ask why. Instead, she sent garments to clothe Mordecai and take away his sackcloth (4:1-3). Servants are very loyal and trustworthy, particularly with leaders. When Esther found out about a plan to kill King Ahasuerus, she exposed the plot, thus saving his life (2:22-23).

Servants wrestle with issues of self-worth and tend to regard others as more worthy than themselves. Servants tend to feel unqualified for spiritual leadership. Esther had a low estimation of her ability to influence the king. When Esther heard Mordecai's words stating, "Yet who knows whether you have come to the kingdom for such a time as this?", she set aside her legitimacy issues and began to rise to her God-given position of authority (4:9-11).

Servants have a high loyalty when it comes to family. When Mordecai was persuading Esther to rise up, he used Esther's loyalty to her family name to persuade her (4:12-14). Servants focus their energy on bringing life to others and empowering them to achieve their best. Their greatest fulfillment is in knowing they enable somebody else to do their work. The actions of Esther empowered Mordecai and the Jewish people. Although Esther's plea before King Ahasuerus ultimately saved them, she stepped aside and let Mordecai and the Jewish people take the spotlight (Esther 8-9).

Teacher

- Needs to validate truth for himself. It is at the core of who he is. Loves knowledge.

- Does not receive new things immediately. Looks at things from different angles.

- Wants first-hand details. Values precision in sharing details. Sometimes overkill of details.

- Processes and makes decisions slowly. Can slow down impulsive people who jump to conclusions.

- Is a very safe person emotionally and is sometimes confused with the gift of mercy. The difference is the teacher tends to be led by their head and mercy to be led by their heart.

- Has a deep commitment to family and tradition.

- Seen as safe because he is patient with those in sin. He is willing to lay out the whole picture and allow the other person to choose to do what is right and be reconciled.

- Resists using personal stories and illustrations when speaking or preaching. Prefers dealing with pure doctrine in a theological way. Loves Greek and Hebrew.

- Tends to be unwilling to begin a process until he can see the end of the process.

- Can be immobilized by fear or risk. It can keep him from obeying God.

- Has a wonderful sense of humor.

- Tends to be the last one to speak in a group. He will listen and observe, seeing things from all angles, then summarize the whole picture.

- Does not reject new ideas immediately. Does not go forward as quickly as visionaries think he should. *above*

- Tends not to take the initiative to confront what is wrong. Can be too tolerant of sin.

- Prefers the old, established, validated ways. Preserves history.

- Looks for more validation. Seeks out more credentials to attest to his competence.

- Tends to feed his mind, more than his spirit. There may be perceived dryness as he dispenses truth with intricate details.

- Tends toward selective responsibility. Can be extremely responsible and reliable in one area, but does not carry that same behavior over to other areas.

- Is unwilling to impose responsibility on others. Finds it difficult to compel someone to do what is right. His natural tendency is to explain, reason and put forth truth, expecting or hoping the other person will pick up the truth and act on it voluntarily.

26

□ Is not easily swayed from the truth. Can keep the more impulsive gifts in check. Serves as an anchor.

 □ Wants to verify truth with his natural wisdom. May lead to struggle with intellectual pride.

□ Can have difficulty with emotions because of a desire to rationalize, explain, and systematize how he feels.

□ Relies heavily on knowledge. Thinks that knowledge is the inside track, and if he has knowledge, he has intimacy. Thinks the more he knows about God, the closer he is to God.

Major Weaknesses

□ Passive. Unwilling to impose responsibility on others. Can be soft on sin and too patient with people who are doing wrong.

□ Struggles with issues of timeliness and responsibility in selective areas. Procrastinates on practical things.

□ Wants to live by sight, not by faith. Wants to know the end of a process before he begins.

□ Intimacy and prayer may be a major battle for the teacher. Tends to pursue a doctrinal system rather than intimacy with his Father.

Biblical Example Of Teacher — Luke

The teacher has a compulsion to validate truth. Luke carefully explained his reasons for writing (Luke 1:1-4). The teacher establishes truth by firsthand investigation. Luke had to go to the primary source for perfect understanding (Luke 1:3). The teacher tends to validate new truth with established truth. Luke connected the present with the past and at points referred back to the prophet Isaiah (Luke 2:25-38; 3:4; 3:23; Acts 1:1). The details of historical accuracy are important. Luke used six historical references to establish when the birth of Jesus happened, when one would have been sufficient (Luke 2:1-5; 3:1-2). He recorded that Jesus was 30 years old when he began his ministry (Luke 1:23). The teacher values systematic sequence in events reported. Luke wrote the fullest and most orderly narrative of the life of Jesus and the early church (Luke 1:3; Acts 1:1).

For the teacher, background is important to the whole picture. Luke gave the back story, whereas Mark began his gospel with John the Baptist (Luke 1-3:19). The teacher values firsthand information and eyewitness accounts, therefore Luke joined Paul on his missionary journeys (Acts 16:10). A teacher does not give an opinion without a thorough thought process. Luke highlighted the way Mary, the mother of Jesus, pondered things in her heart (Luke 1:39-56; 2:19,51). A teacher is a safe person for the marginalized people in the culture. Luke showed that Jesus valued all kinds of people. He wrote more about women, the sick, the poor, tax collectors, sinners, and outcasts like the Good Samaritan (Luke 4:18-19; 5:12-13; 8:1-3; 10:30-37; 13:10-17; 15:11-32; 16:22; 17:11; 23:27,43).

27

Exhorter

- Has the ability to cross every kind of barrier (social, racial, economic, religious) and relate to people wherever they are.

- Is horizontal in his focus and intensely people-oriented. Has never met a stranger.

- Has the ability to share his faith easily and in difficult situations.

- Has a big vision for reaching the world. Most world-changers in world and religious history were exhorters.

- Is capable of having disagreements without alienating others.

- Is skilled in creating and sustaining relationships at all costs.

- Enjoys being around people. Is extroverted, outgoing, a party looking for someplace to happen.

- Is a master communicator. Teaches from real life examples and is very practical.

- Does teamwork well. Is a great networker.

- Is very flexible and quick to see opportunities. Is willing to abandon their plan to go for a new opportunity.

- Is not intimidated by new ideas and new truth.

- Is a visionary. Tends to see a broader picture, the largest number, etc.

- Can seem superficial due to their light-hearted attitude and ability to work a crowd.

- Tends to govern by relationship, persuasion, and majority opinion of people, not by principle.

- Tends to start things and move on.

- Is attuned to the feelings of people and the timeframe needed for them to embrace a new idea.

- Is tactful and able to speak to people in a gracious way to bring them along.

- Is a master of reconciliation.

- Is concerned with communicating God to people. Gets to know who God is, then communicates him to people.

- Will open his heart and be vulnerable in order to open the hearts of others.

- Struggles with a lack of discipline with time.

- Has wonderful intentions, but often falls short in the tyranny of the urgent.

28

- ☐ Sees spiritual lessons in personal pain and suffering.

- ☐ Struggles with not being willing to risk offense, alienation, or rejection. The immature exhorter is unwilling to confront sin. A righteous exhorter will hold a high standard of holiness and bring those around him to that same standard.

- ☐ Works hard and is intensely busy. Functions on little sleep. Is involved in many projects.

- ☐ Can surround himself with people willing to cover for his weaknesses.

Major Weaknesses

- ☐ People-pleasing. Unwilling to confront because of fear of rejection.

- ☐ Poor time management. Tends to take on too much.

- ☐ Compromise. May settle for doing what is good, instead of God's best.

Biblical Example Of Exhorter — Paul

Exhorters can reconcile diversity in a community. A good example is Paul, who worked with all kinds of people (1 Cor 3:1-3; 9:19-23). All of 1 Corinthians 7-8 is instruction on how to relate to others in regard to marriage relationships, singleness, unbelieving spouses, circumcision, slavery, food sacrificed to idols, and weaker brothers. Righteous exhorters become all things to all men in a good sense, but others can be carnal and superficial. Paul related to diverse people for the gospel (1 Cor 9:9,20-23). An exhorter's biggest challenge is not being a slave of popularity. Paul repeatedly argued that he was not a people-pleaser or seeking his own good, but that he followed Christ (1 Cor 4:3-4; 1:17-31; 3:4-5, 21-23; 7:23; 10:31-33; 2 Cor 4:5-6). Exhorters do teamwork and networking well. Paul enlisted a network of support that spread the message widely. He was always talking about his teammates (1 Cor 3:6-9; 16:19-20; 2 Cor 1:11; 13:11; 8:22-24). Paul lead by consensus, persuasion, and appeal (1 Cor 8:8-11; 10:1-2; 13:10).

Exhorters desire to start things and move on. Paul continually went to new places to start churches (1 Cor 3:10). Righteous exhorters hold a high standard of holiness. Paul called for a high standard of holiness and corrected immorality that the Corinthian church was condoning (1 Cor 3:16-17; 5:1-13; 6:13-20; 7:1; 11:27-29). Exhorters can be sensitive to criticism from within the group. Paul repeatedly defended his ministry and apostleship to his critics (1 Cor 9:3; 2 Cor 1:12; 6:3; 8:20-21; 11:5-33; 12:1-21). Paul defended his wisdom from God (1 Cor 2:6-16). Exhorters can take a conciliatory tone on controversial subjects. Paul used persuasion in making his arguments, not authority (1 Cor 12:1,7,11).

Exhorters teach practically, from real life examples. For Paul, it was important that people understand what he was trying to say (2 Cor 1:8-10,13-14,23). Paul opened his heart to open the hearts of others (2 Cor 6:11-13). Paul's passion was to receive from God and communicate him to people (1 Cor 11:23). Paul had a big vision for the world and could get others to share the vision and his values (2 Cor 10:15-16; 8:16-18).

Giver

The giver is the most difficult to peg by behavioral characteristics. Givers are legendary for diversity, adaptability, and flexibility. They do not fit easily into nice, neat pigeonholes.

- Has a generational worldview. Is focused on trying to prepare the way for his family and others after him.

- Is nurturing. Creates a family environment to foster relationships.

- Has a heart for sharing their faith, but tends not to do it personally. Wants to empower others to do the work of evangelism.

- Is very independent. Stands alone. Does not look to other people for help and sometimes not even to God.

- Resists being conned, manipulated, or guilt-tripped into action. Tendency to feel manipulated when others withhold information from him.

- Is able to relate to a wide range of people.

- Desires to empower other people's productivity.

- Desires to keep his own life private.

- Is not confrontational by nature.

- Is keen at finding unseen options, solutions, and resources.

- Is opportunistic in seizing an available moment.

- Finds favor in terms of money. Resources flow to him.

- Gives well and wisely, not impulsively.

- Tends to be frugal with family members which can cause friction.

- Tends to find bargains, good deals, or discounts before making purchases.

- May tend to see money as a source of security.

- Lives in the present and future. Tends not to learn from the past. Does not like to be confronted on issues that are more than a week old.

- Likes to keep all options open as long as possible. Hesitates to accept absolutes in circumstances, maybe even in the Bible.

- Is a natural networker. Has an ability to bring people together and persuade them to do things.

- Is pragmatic and practical.

- Is a peacemaker. Can work with people who have conflicting views and theologies. Can sustain ideological tension in a group or project. Provides a place of safety.

- Is involved in a diversity of projects, interests, and activities. Is multi-focused.

- Can birth, nurture, and protect new things and new ideas. New things arise and grow at a greater pace than other gifts.

- Can struggle with gratitude due to present focus and short memory.

- Does spiritual things, but sometimes not from the right motivation.

- May avoid risk because of a tendency to rely on self rather than God's resources. Faith may seem hard for the giver.

Major Weaknesses

- Independence. Does not need others. May not acknowledge needs to God.

- Hypocrisy. May appear to do the right things, but may not deeply pursue holiness.

- Control and manipulation. Desires to control based on fear of the unknown and risk. Tries to manipulate God and people.

Biblical Example Of Giver — Job

The giver's focus is not solely on his own generation; he intentionally tries to prepare the way for his family after him. Job offered sacrifices for his family (Job 1:5). A giver does God's work with the resources that he receives from God, recognizing that God is his source. Job said, "The Lord gives, and the Lord takes away. Blessed be the name of the Lord." Job understood how to be a steward of God's funds to minister to the needs of the community. He provided for the poor, the widow, the fatherless, and the stranger (Job 31:16-23,32). A righteous giver does not put his trust in money. Job said that his security was not in gold (Job 31:24-26). The giver recognizes that God gives him responsibility in the community. He is a steward in abstract things like wisdom or favor and tangible things like money for the needy. Job had the intangible wealth of influence in the community (Job 1:2; 29:7-11,21-25).

The giver's life is to be characterized by stewardship before God in every way. Job lived in high justice, high holiness, and great ethical behavior in everything that he did (Job 1:8; 29:14-17). The battlefield for the giver is putting himself at risk and allowing God to intervene. The virtue that is the opposite of that stronghold is faith to believe that God knows what he is doing. When Job had lost everything but his life, he did not understand or like what God was doing, but he maintained that God had a right to do what he was doing because he was God (Job 1:21; 42:2-6). God is not interested in how much money a giver can accrue. God wants to establish a relationship with the giver through his supernatural intervention in his life (Job 16:20-21; 29:4). When a giver is living in good stewardship, he recognizes that his life is in God's hands, and he can take it whenever he wishes. When Job was sitting on the ash heap of his life, he said, "Though He slay me, yet will I trust Him" (Job 13:15 NKJV).

31

Ruler

- Thrives under pressure and puts the people around him under the same pressure. This can be either motivational or abusive.

- Is skilled at time management. Controls his time and gets the job done.

- Can be loose on ethics when the end justifies the means.

- Does not ask "why" questions.

- Pulls together a group based on loyalty to the mission. Causes the group to own a problem together.

- Can value loyalty more than competence per se.

- Can use imperfect people and draw the best out of them without allowing their brokenness to damage the goal of a project or group.

- Takes a vision and puts together an effective plan. Is an implementer, not a visionary.

- Is not into blaming himself or others. Wants to figure out how to fix it when something goes wrong.

- Is an empire-builder. Wants to make anything bigger and better.

- Doesn't look to others for solutions. Owns his own problems. Does not look for help.

- Focuses on the immediate task.

- Is not easily distracted from a task.

- Can be task-oriented and fall short in nurturing, shepherding, and correcting what is spiritually wrong.

- Involved in all kinds of projects. Enjoys diversity.

- Does not need the affirmation of other people when he has made up his mind.

- Can do a disproportionate amount of work with the given resources.

- Struggles with doing things in his own strength versus relying on God's power and plan.

- Takes on more tasks than is normally possible to complete in the time that he has.

- Can struggle with proper focus. Is he doing the thing that God called him to do, or is he just doing things to stay busy?

- Is willing to be vindicated by God, and not man.

- Can withstand strong opposition.

32

Major Weaknesses

- Insensitivity. Since he is goal-oriented, he may fail to nurture those around him and may apply pressure without moderation.

- Ethics and integrity. The end justifies the means.

- Compromise. Settling for his agenda instead of God's agenda.

Biblical Example Of Ruler — Nehemiah

The story of Nehemiah provides a great example of the ruler gift. The ruler gravitates to positions of responsibility. Nehemiah held a high position as the cupbearer to the king (Nehemiah 1:11). The ruler gets the big picture of how to repair a broken situation. Nehemiah listened to the reports about Jerusalem and knew what needed to be done to repair the walls (1:2-3; 2:5). Nehemiah had the ability to know what resources were needed to accomplish the task and gathered them (2:4,7-9). He did not need the affirmation of others when he had made up his mind. He withstood strong opposition (2:10,19-20; 4:1-9). Nehemiah knew what to delegate and what to do himself (2:11-15; 4:18b; 7:1-3; 13:11,19,30). He pulled together a diverse team to own a problem (2:16-18; 3:1-32; 4:6).

The ruler can use imperfect people to do a large and complex project. Nehemiah used priests, Levites, goldsmiths, perfume-makers, rulers, women, home owners, merchants, temple servants, city people, and country people to rebuild the wall (3:1-32). He brought together a team based on loyalty, and the people worked with all their heart (4:6). Nehemiah worked people very hard to accomplish the goal (4:21-23) and met every obstacle with practicality. When the people were afraid of being attacked and did not want to continue the work on the wall, Nehemiah armed the people and set up an alarm system with trumpets to warn of danger so that they could continue to work (4:9-18). He required loyalty from Jews who were taking advantage of the situation, thus freeing the people to complete the job without hindrance (5:1-13).

A mature righteous ruler does things by God's strength, although his natural talents and gifts are impressive. Nehemiah did not rely on his own strength but prayed to God for wisdom and strength (1:4-11; 2:4,8,18,20; 4:4-5,9,14-15; 6:9b,16). One of the battlefields of the ruler is choosing to do his own plans versus choosing to do God's plans. Nehemiah did what God had put into his heart to do for Jerusalem (2:12; 7:5). A righteous ruler is not easily distracted from the God-given task. Nehemiah was completely absorbed in the task because of reverence for God (6:2-4; 5:15b-16,19). A ruler gets results disproportionate to the time and resources spent on a project. The wall was completed in 52 days (6:15). Nehemiah was willing to be vindicated by God, and not man. He ended with a cry to God for vindication (13:14,22,29,31).

Mercy

- Gets along with everybody easily. Rarely has enemies.

- Is admired and respected.

- Is a safe person for those who are wounded. Can make everyone feel safe sharing their hurts. Can be approached by complete strangers.

- Can take initiative toward wounded ones. Knows who is feeling rejected or wounded.

- Has a huge number of acquaintances and people who enjoy him but only a few who are close friends. Shares everything with intimate friends.

- Craves intimacy of soul and physical touch. Desires hugs and physical contact.

- Tends to be slow to make transitions based on emotional processing. Does not like rapid change without time to process.

- Hears from God but has difficulty explaining the "why." Operates on subjective and intuitive feelings.

- Makes decisions based on his heart.

- Hates to confront. Wants to keep people from hurting and protect them from pain.

- Does not like to choose sides between two people. Does not want to say one is right and one is wrong.

- Prone to appear indecisive because he does not desire to hurt anybody. Having to choose between people's opinions can be paralyzing.

- Can become a people-pleaser and enabler. The immature mercy may do whatever is necessary to make people around him happy with him.

- May attract abuse and exploitation because of his kindness, niceness, and willingness to allow injustice to happen.

- Has a deep strain of anger, which appears rarely and usually in the context of loyalty to someone else. Tends to take up an offense for a third party.

- Is drawn to gift of prophet. Opposites attract: decisiveness of prophet balances the indecisiveness of mercy. Prophet needs the softening influence of mercy.

- Prone to stubbornness. May acknowledge that what he's doing is not God's will and yet not change. Can choose to be life-giving when he wants to, how he wants to, and where he wants to, but can stubbornly resist doing all the things that God has called him to do.

- Can easily enter into the presence of God. Has a predisposition to worship.

- Often has not resolved the fathering issues in his life.

- May see all pain as bad. May flee pain and keep others from the discipline of God when he intends to build maturity and wholeness through discipline.

Major Weaknesses

- Impurity. Desire for intimacy and physical touch may lead to impurity.

- Enabling. Wants to protect others from pain.

- Compromise. Willing to live with mixture of holy and unholy without calling people to do what is right.

- Non-confrontational. May tolerate abuse and exploitation because he is willing to allow injustice to continue.

Biblical Example Of Mercy — John

The apostle John is a beautiful example of the mercy gift. A mercy has ability to sense genuine love. John uses the word *love* more than any other writer in the Bible (the books of John and 1,2,3 John, especially 1 John 2:5; 3:1,11,14,16-18,23; 4:7-12,16-21; 5:1-3; 2 John 6; 3 John 1,6). A mercy speaks the language of love. John often used terms of relationship and endearment in his letters (1 John 2:1,7,12-14,18; 3:2,7,13,18; 4:1,4,7; 5:21; 2 John 5; 3 John 1,2,5,11). A mercy needs deep friendships with mutual commitment and is drawn to the gift of prophet. John spent a lot of time with Peter who had the gift of prophet (John 19:26; Mark 14:33; Luke 22:8; Acts 3:1-11; 4:13-19; 8:14; Matthew 17:1). A mercy wants physical closeness and quality time (2 John 12). John was frequently found next to Jesus (Matthew 17:1; John 13:23; Mark 10:35-37; 13:3; 14:33; Luke 8:51; 1 John 1:1,3).

A mercy measures relationships by love. John identified himself as the disciple Jesus loved (John 19:26; 20:6; 21:7; 21:20). John valued fellowship in relationships (1 John 1:3; 2:24,27; 3:1,24; 5:19-20). A mercy tends to take up an offense for someone they love. John was fiercely protective of Jesus and his ministry (Mark 9:38; Luke 9:54). A mercy tends to be sensitive to the emotional needs of others. John wrote about emotional needs, such as fellowship, joy, love, fear, torment, and confidence (1 John 1:4; 3:11,14-18,21; 4:7-12,18; 5:14; 2 John 4). A mercy tends to be a follower and not given to boldness, until pushed in a corner. John did not want to be a leader, but when he was challenged he would rise to the occasion. (Acts 4:13,19). A mercy is concerned with the heart message, not the head. John frequently spoke of people's hearts (1 John 3:20-22; 5:10; Rev 1:3). Worship comes easily for a mercy. John wrote the magnificent worship scenes in Revelation (Rev 4:1-11; 5:1-14; 15:2-4; 19:1-10; 22:8-9).

Designed For Fulfillment

Still Not Sure Who You Are?

For most people their dominant redemptive gift jumps off the page at them. For others, it is easily narrowed down to a few, but then a final determination is not so obvious. Sometimes determining a person's redemptive gift is like looking at an uncut gem. To the untrained eye, it looks like a rock. But if one takes the time to remove the excess layers that have been placed on it over time, the true jewel inside begins to emerge. In thinking about the characteristics of the redemptive gifts, it is important to look at what is learned or acquired behavior versus the essence of who and what God designed. The following factors are some of the things that will influence how the redemptive gifts are expressed in a person's life.

Parenting

Every child's parents have their own redemptive gifts. Their gifts impact how they view the world and how they raise their children. Therefore, the parents' gifts will leave a very significant imprint on the children, regardless of what the child's own gifts are. Also, the potential character weaknesses of a parent's gifting can impact the child as well. If a child's parents are servant and exhorter, for example, the child may grow up in a home where the exhorter is financially irresponsible and is living in denial. In an attempt for the servant parent to help meet the child's need, the irresponsible behavior by the exhorter parent may be reinforced by the servant, thereby skewing the proper redemptive gift qualities of the child. Thus, the child may grow up lacking the knowledge needed to be financially responsible, although it is part of their God-given design to want to be a good steward of resources, especially if their redemptive gift is giver. On the positive side, let's look at a child who has the redemptive gift of prophet and is raised by an exhorter. Prophets tend to have difficulty relating to people. Since the exhorter's strength is the ability to maintain relationship with others, the child will most likely be much more relationally oriented than others with the gift of prophet. Because they learned relational skills from their parent, the prophet has the imprint of the parent's exhorter gifting.

Birth Order

Studies have shown for years that there are distinct imprints on a child's personality based on where they are in the birth order. Firstborn children tend to be more driven and perfectionistic by nature. The baby of the family is naturally much more relational and horizontally focused. But that does not mean that all firstborns are gift of prophet, and all babies of the family are exhorters. Being firstborn can intensify all the strengths and weaknesses of any gift (double the good, double the challenges).

Maturity

Everyone is at a different level of maturity in their personal development and Christian life. A person's level of maturity will color how they live the characteristics of their redemptive gift. Those who are immature or are not seeking to live in the fruit of the Spirit will exhibit the weaknesses of their gifts more than the strengths. While nobody has reached perfection, we should all be working on our character issues to grow up to maturity.

Gender

There are several issues regarding gender and redemptive gifts. It is easy to stereotype certain gifts, such as prophet, ruler, and teacher, as being more masculine and servant and mercy as being more feminine. Men often reject the idea of being a mercy or servant because they perceive it as being weak. This is a misconception. The gifts of servant and mercy have some of the strongest spiritual authority. Women with the gifts of prophet and ruler often find it hard to be accepted, validated, and nurtured in a church setting because of the natural boldness and strength of the gifts. Both men and women need to dig deeper in order to see the beauty of what God has designed, instead of trying to be something other than who God made them to be.

Woundedness

Everyone has experienced painful situations and relationships that have left them wounded. Many times those wounds change our perception of ourselves and of God. For example, someone who grew up with an abusive authority figure may become very self-sufficient and independent because they believe they have to make it through life on their own. This is a very different motivation than the God-given independence of the prophet and giver. How we are broken, the pain in our soul, our wrong response to pain, the coping mechanisms, and how we compensate for those wounds will influence how our gift is expressed. Sometimes people build walls of self-protection as a way of surviving painful circumstances. These self-protecting walls may not reflect our gift and may hinder its God-intended expression.

Left-Brain vs. Right-Brain

Whether a person is right-brain or left-brain is an organic issue. Right-brained people see the whole picture. They are generally more creative and emotional, because emotional concepts and messages are stored in the right half of the brain. Left-brained people see the various parts, process logically and in a linear fashion, and think more strategically. Most people have a fairly effective blend between the two sides of the brain and can transition between them with ease, while some people are dominated by one side or the other. Each of the gifts will be expressed differently, depending on whether the person is right-brained or left-brained. A left-brained teacher will look different from a right-brained teacher. A left-brained teacher will be more analytical and research-oriented, will compartmentalize, and will break down information into bite-sized pieces, but right-brained teachers will express their gift more emotionally and more relationally. Left-brained teachers enjoy spending hours researching in the lab or in the library, and right-brained teachers love to be in the classroom and light up when the students "get it." Some of the gifts tend more toward being left-brained in their basic God-given essence and in their expression, like prophet and ruler, which tend to be better at being logical, prioritizing, making decisions, and organizing. The servant gift is more right-brained and therefore may tend to be more emotional and expressive through actions, rather than vocally. The mercy gift is more right-brained, visual, creative, and inclined to the arts and worship. A mercy or servant raised and taught in a left-brained environment may have suppressed those parts of their design that were not seen as acceptable, or they may have acquired organizational skills from watching the parents, but that does not alter the spiritual DNA of their gift.

37

Culture And Time Frame

The family, community, and time in history in which a person lives can have a radical impact on how they perceive themselves and express their gift. The redemptive design is often revealed as a person is able to experience events and challenges that make their heart and spirit come alive. But if you are a woman with a gift of ruler who lives in a culture or time when women should be seen and not heard, there will be a large reservoir of untapped potential because you were not given an opportunity to shine. Your nation and family of origin also have an impact. Your family and your community or country have made you a certain way because that's what they needed or what was accepted. If you were raised in a nation with a redemptive gift of prophet (such as the United States or Germany*), you will have natural affinity for more of the characteristics of prophet, because it is what your culture affirms and cultivates. But this does not mean that your redemptive gift is prophet.

* Cities and nations also have redemptive gifts and will be explored later in this book in the section titled "The Bigger Picture."

Questions To Think About If You Are Still Unsure Of Your Dominant Redemptive Gift

- What about the list of behavior characteristics causes you to believe you are that gift?

- Is it the weaknesses or the strengths?

- If it is the strengths, do you see those things in your life presently, or are they things that you wish were in your life?

- If it is the weaknesses, what are other possible reasons that those weaknesses could be present?

- Have you asked God and given him time to show you?

In-Depth Study

Definition Of Terms And Concepts

Now it is time to take a more in-depth look at each of the seven redemptive gifts. While the natural tendency would be to focus only on the section concerning your dominant redemptive gift, keep in mind that the key principles and concepts in these sections apply to everybody. Everyone has some of all seven of the gifts in different proportions, although one is generally dominant. The ultimate goal is to become more like Christ, who is the perfection of all seven gifts. Everyone must strive to grow in all seven areas. There are several terms and concepts that are critical to the study of redemptive gifts. Please take the time to read the definitions and explanations of these concepts.

Principle

A principle is a universal, non-optional, fundamental, primary, or general law of truth that God has set into motion. A principle is a cause-effect relationship. Man does something, and there is a predictable result according to God's purposeful design. God does not have to intervene to make it happen. The best known example from Scripture is the principle of sowing and reaping. The Bible says that you will reap what you sow (naturally and spiritually), and the amount you will reap will be a direct result of how much you sow (Luke 6:38, Galatians 6:7-9). It is a principle that God has put into motion in both the natural and the spiritual world. It applies in every culture and to every redemptive gift and it applies to the saved and unsaved alike. Regardless of where someone is in their spiritual relationship with God, the principle works because it is part of God's design.

A principle is different from moral law, which deals with behaviors that incur judicial consequences. Justification removes the penalty and condemnation from believers, but it does not automatically rebuild their life. Many people who have experienced salvation still find that their finances, health, relationships, and identity are in all manner of brokenness. Their problems do not necessarily change instantly at the moment of salvation. The new believer does not necessarily receive instant wealth, health, and healing of all emotional scars at salvation. The majority of brokenness needs to be repaired through the application of principles after condemnation and justification have been dealt with through salvation in Christ. Christianity offers principles that produce change and help us possess our birthright. It is God's design for all Christians to learn how to grow into Christ by seeking out the principles of God's Word, principles that bring healing, life, and love.

Proverbs 9:1 says, "Wisdom has built her house, she has hewn out its seven pillars." In this scripture, the seven pillars parallel the seven redemptive gifts outlined in Romans 12:6-8. God gave gifts to the body of Christ in order to help build together a "house" in whom the habitation of the Spirit dwells (Ephesians 2:21-22). The faith community is the "house of God," and the seven pillars represent the seven redemptive gifts represented by individuals in the body of Christ.

By studying what the seven redemptive gifts reveal about God and his wisdom in other portions of Scripture, we have summed up God's wisdom into seven primary principles. For each gift there is a specific set of principles to master. With the right set of principles, the Christian life transforms itself from a position of due diligence — merely doing what we know we ought to do — to a position of freedom, delighting in God's creative ways. The principles in order are:

Prophet — Principle of Design
Servant — Principle of Authority
Teacher — Principle of Responsibility
Exhorter — Principle of Sowing and Reaping

Giver — Principle of Stewardship
Ruler — Principle of Freedom
Mercy — Principle of Fulfillment

We must be passionate in our pursuit of the principles because we desire to grow, not because we are trying to purchase God's acceptance. To the degree that we sow these principles wisely into our lives, we will reap more freedom and live with greater joy and fulfillment.

Authority

There are four different kinds of spiritual authority. People are most familiar with the governmental authority of the church. There is also the positional authority that all believers have because we are seated with Christ Jesus at the right hand of God (Ephesians 2:4). A third kind is the personal gifting designated by God of authority over specific things or situations. The fourth one is the earned authority of demonstrating specific virtues that are the opposite of an iniquity. For example, the servant's weakness is to default to living like a victim. When the servant chooses to live in the opposite virtue of dominion and is life-giving to those around them, that is earned authority. For each of the gifts there is an area of authority that is earned as they choose to live in righteousness. The areas of authority given for each gift are drawn from the day of creation that parallels each redemptive gift.

Birthright

Our birthright is the revelation of what God put in our spiritual DNA. Understanding who God designed us to be and what he made us to do is the pathway to fulfilling our birthright. Solomon was a successful man but did not fulfill his birthright. He had the resources and wisdom to evangelize the world, but instead he used his great fame, power, wealth and unparalleled wisdom to satisfy his own desires. The ultimate fulfillment of God's wisdom would have been for Solomon to make God known in the world, instead of himself, so that the Queen of Sheba would have come to see the splendor of God, not of Solomon's kingdom. According to the book of Ecclesiastes, Solomon eventually recognized the vanity of living without fulfilling God's ultimate design. He died frustrated and in futility. When we do what we were designed to do, we will be dangerous to the kingdom of darkness and be fulfilled in our own Christian life. It is an act of worship to experience fulfillment while pursuing our God-given birthright. Apart from God, man is utterly depraved. Although man with his sin nature is capable of some depraved things,

God's original blueprint that he designed is a masterpiece. The fact that there is sin, pain, woundedness, defilement, demons, and curses affecting God's masterpiece does not change the fact that there is a masterpiece in each person. We fulfill our birthright when we discover who we are and enjoy life in God while pursuing his design for our identity, legitimacy, authority, and abilities. The birthright of each of the gifts is drawn from the description of the seven churches in Revelation that parallel the seven gifts.

The Number Line For The Scale Of Responsibility

Everyone operates in their redemptive gift at different levels of maturity and authority. The Bible urges us to live a life worthy of our calling and to continually be conformed more into the likeness of Christ (Romans 12:2; 2 Corinthians 3:18). In Ephesians 4:23, Paul says to put off the old ways and to "be made new in the attitudes of our minds and put on the new self, created to be like God in true righteousness and holiness." Picture life as a number line going from –100 to +100. What does living at +100 look like? Is it merely living a good life and striving for an absence of sin? Ephesians 4:28 says, "He who has been stealing must steal no longer, but must work, doing something useful with his own hands, that he may have something to share with those in need." According to Paul, refraining from the sin of stealing is only a beginning point. If a person stops stealing, he is only at 0 on the number line. Making enough money to cover his own costs so as not to take from others would be a bit a higher in plus numbers, but he should strive for even more, enough to give to others.

For each redemptive gift there is a number line for its specific scale of responsibility, outlining what the gift looks like when it is operating from –100 to +100. The number line attempts to describe the process of change in terms of bondage at –100, obedience at 0, and freedom at +100. On the number line –100 is bondage, when our willpower is not sufficient to control our behavior. 0 is obedience when we have enough willpower not to sin, but obedience in itself brings no pleasure. Obedience is not the goal but a point to go through on the way to freedom. Total freedom is +100. Christ did not come to compel us to obey; he came to give us the truth that sets us free from within. Most believers do not live in that level of freedom, but are living in obedience with a significant amount of "white-knuckle" willpower invested in doing what is right. As an overview of the principle of scale of responsibility, the points on the number line in general for all the gifts are illustrated on the next page.

+ 100 The integration of the redemptive gifts of people groups, the principles of the Word of God, and the seasons of God's moving.

+ 80 Bringing healing to an entire group of people who are not seeking to be healed or changed, reconciling and releasing them into God's design for them.

+ 60 Reconciling, releasing, and empowering individuals who are not seeking to be changed. +60 is achieved when someone has the spiritual authority to cut through demonic bondage and the skill and emotional level to help angry, wounded people. They have the skill to penetrate blindspots and bring healing to those who aren't seeking to be healed.

+40 Represents working with those who are willing to grow and be changed.

+20 Represents making personal moral choices. +20 is the enemy's greatest triumph. Many people arrive at a point of comfort and stop growing. +20 beats –80, but it's still under-achieving.

0 "White-knuckle" obedience, not adding positive virtue but not adding to the iniquity.

- 20 The level of soft choices and compromise that most people make.

- 40 Represents a large portion of the population. The level of sin at –40 adds significantly to the quantity and depth of iniquity in a society by sheer volume.

- 60 Represents a smaller number of the population than –40, but greater than –80.

- 80 Embraces a slightly larger group doing evil than –100. It is higher profile, easier to see and to measure, but still they are not a significant percentage of the population.

-100 Represents very few people of great evil.

Curses And Blessings

The story of humanity is that of a war between life and death, light and darkness, blessings and curses. Repeatedly Scripture states that there is a choice to make. By their words and actions people invoke either the power of light or darkness. Proverbs 18:21 says "The tongue has the power of life and death." In Deuteronomy 30:19-20, God said, "This day I call heaven and earth as witnesses against you that I have set before you life and death, blessings and curses. Now choose life, so that you and your children may live and that you may love the Lord your God, listen to his voice, and hold fast to him."

The principle of blessing was introduced at creation as God blessed what he had made. Tragically, the principle of curses was introduced shortly after that at the Fall. The first recorded curse in the Bible is in Genesis 3:17 NKJV. "Then to Adam He said, 'Because you have heeded the voice of your wife, and have eaten from the tree of which I commanded you, saying, 'You shall not eat of it': "Cursed is the ground for your sake; In toil you shall eat of it all the days of your life." God cursed the earth when Adam and Eve sinned through their disobedience.

A curse is defined as invoking evil on or pronouncing a desire for ill will against someone or some thing. To be under a curse is to actually experience or be under the evil that was invoked or desired. Curses take away the quality of life. They can bring failure, shame, sickness, and even physical death. They are temporal in nature and can cause a lot of grief. Curses due to sin can be administered to get a person's attention and encourage them to turn back to God. Those who humble themselves and repent will find restoration and renewed freedom from the Lord. Those who become angry and self-righteous, rebel, and remain unrepentant go deeper into bondage and darkness.

Generational curses are judgments that are passed on from generation to generation. Generational curses bring judgment or bondage to the next generations. Exodus 34:6-7 NKJV speaks of generational curses. "And the Lord passed before him and proclaimed, 'The Lord, the Lord God, merciful and gracious, longsuffering, and abounding in goodness and truth, keeping mercy for thousands, forgiving iniquity and transgression and sin, by no means clearing the guilty, visiting the iniquity of the fathers upon the children and the children's children to the third and the fourth generation.'"

While the idea of curses is sobering, there is good news. For everything the enemy tries to do to bring death and destruction, there is always more life, light, and power to overcome it. Curses from sin bring judgment, but we are also offered the alternative of blessings. Deuteronomy 11:26-28 NKJV says, "Behold, I set before you today a blessing and a curse: the blessing, if you obey the commandments of the Lord your God which I command you today; and the curse, if you do not obey the commandments of the Lord your God, but turn aside from the way which I command you today, to go after other gods which you have not known." It is true that curses are passed down to the third and fourth generation, but God's mercy flows down for a thousand generations. Exodus 20:5-6 says "I, the Lord your God, am a jealous God, punishing the children for the sin of the fathers to the third and fourth generation of those who hate me, but showing love to a thousand generations of those who love me and keep my commandments."

Wise warriors in this battle must educate themselves about the potential curses so that they know how to bring the blood of Jesus against anything that would attempt to steal, kill, or destroy. Curses can be empowered in several ways. Curses can be spoken words against someone or something that can affect people, even if they are ignorant of it. For example, Joshua uttered a curse against anyone who would try to rebuild the city of Jericho (Joshua 6:26 NASB). Though hundreds of years passed, this curse still carried out its destruction (1 Kings 16:34).

43

Curses can also occur as the result of broken covenant. As things went badly for King David, he suspected something was amiss. God revealed that his predecessor, King Saul, had afflicted the Gibeonites in violation of a treaty made centuries earlier (2 Samuel 21:3-6,9). If someone enters into a covenant or vow, and the vow is broken, the consequences of the covenant are activated. God had David renegotiate a covenant with the Gibeonites. Seeking the Lord will result in finding a solution that will negate a curse.

Some of the most powerful curses passed on to us are from those who love us the most — our family. No one is perfect. We have all fallen short of God's holy standard (Romans 3:23). While there is mercy and grace available to those who want to receive it, God has also set laws into place such as reaping what you sow (2 Corinthians 9:6, Galatians 6:7-8). God wants parents to sow life-giving seeds in the garden of their child's heart. Yet even the best family lines pass down to the next generation not only good seed but bad seed as well.

Imagine that you receive a letter informing you that a relative died and left you a piece of land. You are told that there was a rich deposit of gold in the land. There is only one problem. There is also some toxic waste in portions of the land that need to be cleaned up. What would you do? Would you look at the waste and say, "Forget the gold. There is toxic waste there." No! You would work to have the waste removed so that you might access the rich deposit of gold waiting for you.

Our lives are like that piece of land. God has placed rich deposits in each of us. There are blessings that flow down our family lines from the generations before us. But there are also toxic things that flow down that same family line. It would be foolish not to work to clean up the waste, so that we can enjoy our righteous inheritance. As children of God Most High, we must learn the depths of the rich inheritance of blessings he has for us. We are urged in Luke 6:28 and Romans 12:14 to do the opposite thing that comes naturally for the world. We are commanded to bless those who curse us, allowing our words of life to defeat the darkness.

For each of the seven redemptive gifts there is a particular type of curse and blessing from the Bible. The seven curses are drawn from the seven enemies of Israel in the promised land listed in Judges. The seven blessings are biblical examples of people whose actions were directly opposite of the enemies of Israel. As people have worked through this part of the study, renouncing the curses and asking for the blessings to be released, God has released many people to live in the fullness of what he designed for them.

Life-Giving

What does it mean to be a life-giver? The Scripture has much to say about being life-giving. In the creation account the first woman was named Eve. Eve means "life" or "life-giver." Abraham was told by God that he was blessed to be a blessing (Genesis 12:2). In Exodus, the golden lamp stand stood as a permanent reminder that God is the life-giver. The manna in the wilderness symbolized Christ as a life-giver. In John 6:32 Christ says, "Moses did not give you the bread from heaven, but my Father gives you the true bread from heaven." In John 6:35, Jesus said, "I am the bread of life. He who comes to me will never go hungry, and he who believes in me will never be thirsty." The raising of Lazarus from the dead identified Jesus as the Life-giver. He is the ultimate Life-giver. Jesus revealed this again in John 10:10 when he said, "I have come that they may have life, and have it to the full." He also said, "I am the way, the truth and the life."

Christ came that we could have life so abundant that it overflows from us to others. We are to be so filled with the good news, good fruit, and the Spirit that it affects those around us. The life given to us by Christ becomes life that we share with others. When we are life-givers to others, we let Christ live his life through us. To the degree we hear from the Father as Christ did and say what the Father is saying and do what the Father is doing, we will be fruitful life-givers.

Legitimacy Lie

We are created to leave a legacy. God commanded Adam and Eve and Noah (when the earth was destroyed) to be fruitful and multiply. Jesus also commanded his disciples to leave a legacy when he said, "Go and make disciples of all nations." All of us are called to leave a legacy, but we can become ensnared in a trap when we draw our legitimacy from what we do instead of who we are. God designed us to draw our legitimacy only from him. We are legitimate because we are of the essence of God (Genesis 1:26; Ephesians 2:4-10). What we do doesn't cause God to love us. We are complete in him.

When we do not find our legitimacy in God, we begin to seek it from other people or in accomplishments. As we do that, we begin to believe lies about our legitimacy. We begin to believe we are only legitimate when we do things or obtain certain levels of achievement. No matter which of the redemptive gifts we represent, each of us has a legitimacy lie that we are prone to believe and act upon. These lies are the foundations of the seven curses that can destroy our birthright and calling. We must fight to renounce the legitimacy lies we believe and redesign our beliefs around one truth: My Father designed me the way I am, and he loves the way he designed me. In him I am complete (2 Peter 1:3).

Sevens In Scripture

While anything, including numbers in Scripture, can be taken to an extreme, the facts concerning numbers in the Bible cannot be ignored. There has been no number in the Bible more studied than the number seven. The number seven is significant because it reveals a part of God's character. As an example, in Revelation 1:4, 3:1, and 4:5, John saw seven lamps that represented the seven Spirits of God. The sevens in Scripture point us to God and speak of who he is. There are over 100 lists of sevens in the Scripture.

The correlation and significance of the Scriptural patterns of seven is not used by chance, but rather is present in Scripture by God's design. Therefore, when we speak of the seven redemptive gifts, we suggest that they are inherently connected to the significant number patterns in other portions of God's written Word. Because we can trust that God's Word is in harmony with itself, we can use the numeric wisdom of Scripture to help us understand the seven redemptive gifts. Our approach is to take a list of sevens in the order that it is mentioned in Scripture and draw out information concerning the seven redemptive gifts. Take the seven days of creation. Each day of the creation account reveals something about who God is and brings clarity to understanding one particular redemptive gift. The gifts parallel the days, so the first day of creation corresponds to the gift of prophet, the second day with servant, and so on. Various lists of sevens in the Scripture also contribute to our understanding of redemptive gifts. The study and understanding of redemptive gifts as they relate to the other lists of sevens in Scripture is embryonic at best. You may want to consider those possibilities in Scripture and draw out applications for the Body of Christ to use.

For the purposes of having a deeper understanding of each of the seven redemptive gifts, we will use God's number patterns in the following Scriptural areas: (1) the seven days of creation, (2) the seven items of furniture in the tabernacle of Moses, (3) the seven compound names of Jehovah, (4) the seven last sayings of Christ on the cross, and (5) the seven letters to the churches in Revelation.

Prayer Of Blessing For Each Redemptive Gift

At the end of each section there is a prayer of blessing for the gift. The blessing prayer is a tool we can use for ourselves and others. It is a blessing to agree with God that what he created in us is a masterpiece. The best way to use this resource is to find a partner who will speak this blessing out loud to you. Something significant happens when we are affirmed by another person in our God-given design, weaknesses and strengths alike. Since everyone has some level of all seven of the redemptive gifts active in their life, we recommend praying through all seven of blessings and drawing affirmation from the qualities of each gift that you see in your life or that you want to grow in. The prayers of blessing included are just a model or abbreviated starting point. Look for other characteristics of each gift as you go through this study and create your own prayer of blessing for yourself and those around you.

Prophet

The redemptive gift of prophet takes principles of truth and applies them to solve problems and to explain purpose, plans, design, or strategy. They are re-builders and restorers of what is broken or chaotic. The gift of prophet has a passion for holiness and has a hard time forgiving himself and others. The gift of prophet likes to prod others forward to excellence to be all they can be. Prophets can be fiercely competitive and are motivated by new or seemingly impossible tasks. They tend to gravitate toward the assignments that have a risk of failure if God does not come through. They are most fulfilled when they see someone they have invested in embrace their birthright and become a reproducing disciple. Prophets are drawn to two types of people, those who excel as leaders and the very broken who do not believe they can live in dignity or be used by God. A prophet has a strong ability to see the birthright and calling of both leaders and the broken and call forth the things God has placed in them. God requires a higher price from the prophet than from any other gift. He prunes his life to build a deeper root system, to bring forth more fruit, and to build more authority in his life. The gift of prophet tends to be more ideologically driven than relationally driven. The prophet might withdraw from somebody who is not in agreement or who is opposed to their ideology, rather than resolve that tension. The prophet may tend to separate from other people rather than to embrace the differences and work through them and create healing and wholeness. That is the battlefield for the prophet.

Biblical Examples Of Prophet: Caleb, Elijah, Ezekiel, Miriam, and Peter.

Principle Of Design

The principle of design is the first of the seven principles and parallels the redemptive gift of prophet. The principle of design can be difficult to explain, but it is foundational to all other principles. One way to explain the principle of design is to describe the prophet as the research and development section of the body of Christ. Prophets are at their finest and doing what God created them to do, when they are solving problems through invention or expansion. They can see new applications and new ways to implement God's principles in different situations. It is in the DNA of prophets to take principles from the Word of God and from natural laws and find new tools for rebuilding and healing. Prophets weave principles together in order to produce change.

God created several different levels of principles. For example, there are principles of relationship between man and matter, such as the law of gravity. These are generally called natural laws, and they govern our universe. There are also principles that govern relationships between people, what can be defined as relational laws (e.g., love your neighbor as yourself). There are also principles of relationship between God and man, or the spiritual laws that govern our relationship with God (John 4:23-24; Romans 8:13-14). The prophet can often struggle with relational laws, so their greatest glory is in mastering relationships with others. The challenge for all the gifts is to embrace all the principles, not just the ones that come easily. While prophets are embracing all the principles, they need to do it without watering down the truth that God gives them to speak into people's lives.

Prophets are gifted to help others know who they are and what they are to do because of their inherent ability to recognize God's design, identity, and calling in others. The prophet's insight into God's design is life-giving. Since each person's design is a reflection of the Father, the act of revealing God's design of the individual also reveals the nature of the Father. Prophets weave all of these principles together to speak life, light, and truth.

Authority Of Prophet

- To call things forth by weaving principles together and to speak life, light, and truth into areas.

- High authority over the poverty spirit.

Birthright Of Prophet

- To help others to obtain their birthright and live in their destiny.

- To provide vision and teaching on God's design and principles.

- To inspire/teach others to voluntarily embrace the pain required to obtain their birthright.

Number Line Of The Scale Of Responsibility

+100 **Integration of redemptive gifts of people groups, the principles of the Word of God, and the seasons of God's moving.**

+80 **Bringing reconciliation, empowerment, and release to entire groups.** Understanding strengths, anointing, and needs of entire groups and bringing out the best in all of them based on their calling and gifting.

+60 **Bringing reconciliation, empowerment, and release to those who are unwilling.** Befriending and converting those who come against the church instead of rejecting them (witches, Satanists trying to corrupt the church, etc.).

+40 **Bringing reconciliation, empowerment and release to the severely broken ones who seek help.** Healing victims of abuse, survivors of ritual abuse, the financially broken.

+20 **Seeking spiritual principles and healing for themselves instead of trying to "fix" everyone else.** Looking at and understanding the wounds and blind spots in their own life. Bringing their spirit into dominion over their soul which brings wholeness.

0 **Working with all types.** Embracing pain and working where it is difficult, not just easy. Identifying the missing principle impeding growth for those who are not the easy/normal cases (deliverance, inner-healing, legitimacy).

-10 **Selective Ministry.** Working only when it easy and convenient to work with others. Choosing to only work in ministry or with people where "success" is easily visible.

-20 **Staying in silent tolerance.** People who continue to stay in situations that need reform, despite disagreement and dissatisfaction, but do not actively try to help the situation. Also seen when team members set aside differences for a good cause, but do not enjoy true fellowship with one another.

-40 **Leaving in silent withdrawal.** People who leave when they are dissatisfied instead of staying to try and make it better. Congregations moving locations when the racial makeup of the neighborhood changes instead of staying to make an impact. This empowers the stronghold of social fragmentation and conflict-avoidance instead of being life-giving.

-60 **Ruled by anger.** Victims of injustice, angry wounded people who wound others and continue the cycle. Racial victims and gangs. Parts of the church that bash others.

-80 **Holding to a conviction or theology that justifies fragmentation and alienation.** Groups such as KKK, white supremacists, black supremacists, and anti-Semitic groups.

-100 **Satanic ritual abuse.** Extensive development of knowledge and principles concerned with the breaking or fragmenting of a human being (body, soul, and spirit).

Aramean Curse

Biblical Basis: Genesis 28-29

So Isaac called for Jacob and blessed him and commanded him: "Do not marry a Canaanite woman. Go at once to Paddan Aram, to the house of your mother's father Bethuel. Take a wife for yourself there, from among the daughters of Laban, your mother's brother. May God Almighty bless you and make you fruitful and increase your numbers until you become a community of peoples. May he give you and your descendants the blessing given to Abraham, so that you may take possession of the land where you now live as an alien, the land God gave to Abraham."
Then Isaac sent Jacob on his way, and he went to Paddan Aram, to Laban son of Bethuel the Aramean, the brother of Rebekah, who was the mother of Jacob and Esau (Genesis 28:1-5).

Jacob goes, sees Rachel, and wants to marry her. But Laban tells him he must work for seven years and then he can have Rachel. On the wedding day Laban tricks Jacob, and he marries Leah, not Rachel. Laban said, "It isn't right for my younger daughter to get married before my older one." So Jacob has to work another seven years for Rachel. He loves Rachel, but not Leah. Laban, an Aramean, broke a covenant agreement he had made with Jacob. By giving Jacob Leah instead of Rachel after seven years of work, Laban is seeking illegal and lawless ways to solve his own problem, not trusting that God would provide a husband for Leah. Laban would not let Jacob receive justice by letting him out of the marriage with Leah after the truth was found out.

When we are living like Laban the Aramean, we try to use God to fix things. Lots of prayer seeks to make our will be done, not God's will. We try to harness God to fix things and people the way we think they should be fixed. Freemasonry is the greatest open door to the Aramean curse. It is using ungodly spiritual power to fix things in the business world, judicial system, and family system.

Legitimacy Lie
"I can solve my own problems and fix things better than God. I am legitimate when I fix things."

Signs Of The Curse
- You cannot solve your own problems in the context of civil law.
- You are continually facing legal issues or getting injustice in basic business deals.
- You are misjudged and misrepresented in relationships with others. Others focus on the 1% that is bad about you versus the 99% that is wonderful about you.

Possible Causes
- You or someone in your family line sought lawless power in order to solve their problems.
- You or someone in your family line relied on their own resources, taking justice into their own hands, instead of allowing God to fight their battles.
- You have a generational history of Freemasonry.

50

Prayer Of Renunciation For The Aramean Curse

Father God, I come before your throne in my blood covenant relationship with Jesus Christ. This covenant gives me specific legal rights. I have a legal right to be free from the enemy's curses and control, to possess my God-given birthright, and to reap good things where I have sown good seed. I rejoice that you are the righteous judge of the universe, the Ancient of Days. Open the books in every branch of my family line. Identify every person who has lived in the Aramean curse, every legitimacy lie that they believed, every person who solved a problem that was not theirs, every person who failed to solve a problem that was theirs. Father, cover those events with the blood of the Lord Jesus Christ.

I reject and renounce the legitimacy lie that legitimacy comes from solving problems. I reject and renounce the iniquity of choosing to use occultic power to solve problems. I acknowledge that it was just for these curses to come into my family line. You were just in allowing the enemy to devour my family line because of those wrong choices.

I have a higher legal right in the blood of Jesus Christ which is sufficient to break the power of those curses. Because of my repentance and renunciation, I receive the cleansing that you have promised in your Word. I send those curses to the cross of Jesus Christ. I nail them there, covered with the blood of Christ. Starting at the cross, I bring that cleansing forward in every branch of my family line, from generation to generation, to the present, to my spouse, to my children, and to all my physical and spiritual seed to a thousand generations.

Now because the legal right has been removed through repentance and the application of the blood of Jesus Christ, I command in the name of Jesus of Nazareth that every devouring demon that used to be empowered by the Aramean curse be gone from me, from my family, and from my spiritual and physical seed; from our health, finances, mental capacity, relationships, and spiritual birthright and destiny. I command you to go now where Jesus sends you, never to return.

Most High God, build a fortress of righteousness in the place where the stronghold of darkness used to be. Open my eyes to show me how to live in authority, how to grow in authority, how to make the right choices. Release every blessing that has been held back by the curses. Release the financial blessings, the blessings of favor, and every blessing that has been accrued in heaven that is necessary for me to possess my birthright. I ask these things because you are a just and holy God. I have tasted your justice in the judgment that has been on me, and I anticipate tasting your justice in the restoration that comes from your hand. Thank you in advance in the name of Jesus Christ. I worship you for your holiness and for your love. Amen.

Blessing Of Hosea

The Aramean curse prevents a person from receiving justice in both formal and informal settings. The most important place to receive justice is in the home. Breaking the Aramean curse allows justice, but the blessing of favor is far better than mere justice. Hosea demonstrated that in his relationship with his rebellious wife, Gomer. To get her attention, he had to punish her (Hosea 2:2-13). People are not generally drawn to those who inflict pain on them. Even when they know there is justice involved, they tend to resent the person who inflicts pain. Yet verse 14 says, "I (Hosea) am now going to allure her..." Hosea could box his wife in, and he could break her financially, but he could not coerce her heart. However, God placed such a mantle of favor on Hosea that his calloused, wounded wife turned to him. After disciplining Gomer for her actions, Hosea was able to allure her into a place of intimate love. She followed him willingly and over time allowed him to heal her spirit, soul, and body. She would no longer call him "master" but "husband" (Hosea 2:14-16; Hebrews 12:5-13). Justice broke her, but favor restored her.

Of all the people in Scripture who lived in favor, this blessing is named after Hosea because injustice in the home is the most common area for the Aramean curse to manifest. Having favor in the home that leads to healing a deeply wounded, systematically dysfunctional family is one of the finest manifestations of this blessing. The blessing of Hosea is evident when someone is willing to believe in you beyond what your actions demand. God designed believers to have favor in their family and their community. God entrusts favor to those whom he knows will use it to expand his kingdom, not their own agenda.

Signs Of The Blessing Of Hosea

You have basic security from intrusion in your life. The legal system works for you. You can function within a normal parameter for getting justice. You have favor in the community, government, marketplace, and social situations. There are three basic types of favor or honor you can receive:
1. You receive credibility in your community,
2. Others open a door for you, giving you more than justice, and
3. Those whom you have wounded come back to you for ministry and relationship.

How To Develop In The Blessing Of Hosea

- Cease speaking evil about what you already have. Where has God tried to position you for honor, and you have dismissed it or discredited it?
- Extend favor to others who have not earned it and cannot repay it.
- Sow a lifestyle of showing favor to others. Show favor by making eye contact with others, giving the gift of your time, etc.
- Focus on and celebrate intimacy with God instead of focusing on your achievements.
- Celebrate God's love in the places of your incompetence. Where in your life was your best not good enough, and God showed you his love? Where have you failed and God spoke to you about his love in that moment? People naturally focus on their inadequacies and their perceived rejections by God. Choose to intentionally focus on the opposite.

Sevens In Scripture

Creation

In Scripture the first day of creation parallels the gift of prophet. In Genesis we see that there was a void, chaos, emptiness, and lack of order and structure in the universe. God spoke into the unformed void and said, "Let there be light." Out of God's being came the reality of light in a world that knew no light (Genesis 1:1-3). Day one of God's creation story ultimately parallels the prophetic role of Jesus Christ described in the first chapter of John's gospel. Christ, the prophetic Word of the Father made flesh, brought light into the darkness of humanity (John 1:1-5, 9,18). So too the redemptive gift of prophet (1) recognizes the light of truth that is in the heart and mind of God and speaks it forth, (2) spiritually discerns things that the soul cannot see, (3) understands the abstract principles in the mind of the Father, and (4) receives insights from God that can't be put into words.

On the first day of creation, God created the building blocks from which everything else came. The prophet's job as the first of the seven redemptive gifts is to conceive new things and work with the other gifts to bring them to maturity (Ephesians 2:20). The prophet tends to conceive more than is ever brought to maturity. The prophet will have more creative ideas than he knows what to do with. The design of the prophet is to synchronize with the creativity of God and conceive new things that have never been seen.

Items Of Furniture In The Tabernacle

The first item of furniture in the tabernacle was the brazen altar where sin was dealt with (Exodus 27:1-8; 38:1-7). The people could not go any further toward the presence of God until they dealt with their sin by acknowledging and confessing it and making the sacrifice. God designed the prophet to react to right and wrong. He has the keenest sense for acknowledgment of a wrong and the need for genuine repentance. The prophet is not comfortable with a change in behavior without acknowledgement of sin. God made the prophet to desire that high standard of repentance and to require repentance and confession. In the temple there is no other access to the holiness of God unless you first go by the brazen altar. In the eyes of God it is an essential first step in coming into his presence and knowing him. The prophet's calling is to pursue holiness intensely and challenge others to be holy and confess their unholiness in order to raise the standard of holiness. The prophet is called to bring confession, not condemnation. When sin was confessed and the animal was sacrificed, it was over and done. The prophet is designed to bring closure to issues and encourage the pursuit of intimacy with God.

Compound Names Of Jehovah

The first of the seven compound names is Jehovah-Jireh, "The Lord will provide," found in Genesis 22:13-14. God provided a ram for Abraham to sacrifice, instead of sacrificing Isaac. The brazen altar is the place for the sacrifice for sin. The name Jehovah-Jireh is specific to God providing for a blood sacrifice to cover the sin of man. Like Abraham, God asks us to be willing to sacrifice whatever he asks. Ultimately, only the holiness and righteousness of God can satisfy a holy God. It's the beginning place of our relationship with God. He provides the sacrifice,

53

paying the penalty for our sins. The prophet understands the chasm between the sinfulness of man and the holiness of God. He is intentional about re-establishing and restoring sinful man's relationships with an awesome holy God.

Seven Last Sayings Of Jesus On The Cross

Each of the seven sayings parallels a challenge for a particular redemptive gift. The first thing that Christ said on the cross was "Father, forgive them, for they do not know what they are doing" (Luke 23:34). Christ understood that the crucifixion was planned and that the Father had sent him to earth for this. Therefore, although what the Romans did was illegal, cruel, and wrong, Jesus forgave them and asked his Father to forgive them. Bitterness is a default weakness of the prophet. The passion of prophets for holiness may cause them to take up offense for God in what is wrong and sinful. Prophets must realize that everything that happens is Father-filtered. Painful and unholy things are permitted for his good reasons by a holy, loving Father. If prophets will forgive and embrace the purposes of God without validating what is wrong, God can produce the desired transformation. To the degree that the prophet holds on to bitterness, he blocks God from doing the good that he intends to do through the pain for the prophet and for the kingdom.

Seven Letters To The Churches In Revelation

The redemptive gift of prophet parallels the church of Ephesus in Revelation 2:1-7. ***"I know your deeds, your hard work, your perseverance."*** The Father has wired the prophet to thrive on hard work, to find gratification in it, to persevere, to break through, and to stay with something until there is closure. This can keep them up late into the night until things get done. It is difficult for the prophet to relax and really rest until a project is completed. Every prophet has people telling him he should not be so task-oriented, driven, doing so much. But God celebrates this characteristic of the prophet. ***"I know you cannot tolerate wicked men, and that you have tested those who claim to be apostles but are not and have found them false."*** Prophets are legendary for conflicts with authority figures and are often labeled rebellious or unsubmissive. Prophets are designed to test leadership, reject what is false, and discern which leaders are appointed by God. ***"You have persevered and endured hardships for my name, and have not grown weary."*** Prophets endure pain for the name of Christ. God calls the prophet to bear in their bodies, emotional relationships, ministry, and finances a higher price than the other gifts. That is not a mark of sinfulness or being inferior. He designed the prophet to endure hardship for the cause of Christ. The prophet is willing to defend the reputation and honor of Christ for the gratification that they defended their Lord. ***"To him who overcomes, I will give the right to eat from the tree of life, which is in the paradise of God."*** The tree of life was part of God's design of a culture that would live forever, based on righteousness, godliness, and the unfolding of truth. But the Fall changed everything. We live in a world that is fallen and needs restoration. The prophet is gifted to repair, to find solutions, and to find keys that unlock things. A great portion of the prophet's life is spent repairing what is broken or trying to build over something that has a flawed foundation. God promises that he will reward prophets who work diligently in the redemptive process in this broken season. There is a second chapter coming. You will eat from the tree of life. You will release something that will live forever.

54

Blessing Prayer For Prophet

Prophet, you are a visionary. You are at your finest doing what God created you to do when you are trying to solve problems through discovering principles and applying them. You are called to see new applications and new ways to implement God's principles in new situations. In many things you are the conception point. You easily do vision-casting to get people, especially leaders, to see the call of God on their life and to embrace pain in order to live in their birthright. You can provide the vision to bring a group of people to possess their birthright. You are fulfilled when you can show a picture of God so real that it takes others to the point of excellence in experiencing all that God can do. I bless this inspirational and transformational quality of your gift.

I bless your passion for excellence in yourself and others, especially leaders. You see the fingerprints of God on the broken and come alongside them to restore. You celebrate who the person can become when liberated from their bondage. Your passion for restoration draws you to brokenness, as you see the evil of sin and the restorative power of God. You understand the deep damage done to people and to the kingdom when sin is dealt with lightly. You stand in the gap between what is and what could be. You are quick to say this is wrong, but you know how to wisely handle principles of grace, reconciliation, and rebuilding to restore a broken life.

I bless your fierce intentionality and intensity. Let God sanctify that gift of excellence because he is excellent, so that you don't fall into perfectionism.

I bless your need to be alone. God wants time alone with you for intimacy with him. It is important to give him this first-fruits of your time.

It seems that you are called to pay a higher price than other gifts in your personal disciplines. There are seasons when God seems to be silent in your life. I bless you during these pruning times to build a deeper root system for greater productivity in fruit that remains. In these times God is drawing you up to a higher level. I bless you with making sense of your wilderness experiences, but sometimes you can see it only in hindsight.

I bless your commitment to abstract truth. You demonstrate faith based on the principles of God's Word. "God said it. I believe it. This truth will work. Let's go with it." The fear of the Lord is your stock-in-trade. I bless you with keen, sensitive ears to what God desires, because when you hear from him, you will do it. You often stand like a signpost directing toward the Way, the Truth and the Life to incite others to action, to turn their eyes toward God, and to urge them forward.

You take initiative and enjoy new things. You shift gears quickly, you change from one direction to another. You are active, not passive. Independence is a high value. You are a trail-blazer and pioneer, not a city-dweller. You are a catalyst, not a slow responder. You think outside the box. You hate maintaining the status quo. You know no fear in your basic boldness. You are not intimidated by the unknown or change. I bless your hard work, your persistence, endurance, keeping on keeping on when others would quit. I bless your doing the right thing at great personal cost because it is the right thing to do. I bless your need to have a goal, a reason to live, and an objective. You cannot tolerate having no options. You do not like to be locked into one plan that is not allowed to be improved or changed. You want to make sense out of everything, even unreasonable situations. You don't do well when there is no reason, no point, no progress toward a positive end. You need the "why." I bless you to let God be God at times when he does not choose to tell you the "why."

I bless you to learn to establish appropriate bridges in relationship without compromising truth in order to get truth accepted by relational people. I bless you with patience with earning the right to speak because of relationship, when you believe that truth speaks for itself. As you are willing to embrace relationship, you will speak as God wants you to speak into situations.

You tend to see things in black and white, right and wrong. You hate lukewarm, mediocre, and compromise. I bless that intolerance for mediocrity and shades of gray. Let God temper it with viewing others through the blood of Jesus, who was full of grace and truth. I bless you with the fullness of grace to see beyond win-lose to seek out win-win responses and solutions.

I bless your compulsion for honesty, vulnerability, integrity, and transparency. You are verbally expressive and articulate, often the first to speak in a group. You recoil from hidden agendas, manipulation, and deception. You have keen discernment to quickly assess and evaluate people and situations. You can spot rebels and phonies, especially in leadership. Your first impression is right nine times out of ten. You do not tolerate rebellion, hypocrisy, and denial. You process quickly and have an opinion on everything. Give that discernment to God and ask him what he wants to do with it. I bless you to let God add his measure of grace so that your discernment does not turn to judgment, criticism, and bitterness.

You can build, not just criticize. You can identify a problem, embrace it, and apply the right principle to effectively make things right. You always seek right solutions. I bless your God-given sense of justice to be a champion for people to receive everything that God wants them to have.

You tend to be hard on yourself and are prone to self-condemnation. Your default position is that you messed up or didn't do enough or didn't do it right. I bless you with taking your failures or shortcomings to the throne of grace and there to find mercy in the face of your Father.

I bless your wide range of emotions. You are intense and passionate. Jesus was the essence of joy, but he was called a man of sorrows and spoke with passionate urgency, pity, and anger about religious life in his day. You can experience depression but are also one of the best at celebrating what God has done.

I bless your generosity and loyalty. I bless you with God's wisdom in giving and bestowing loyalty. I bless you with growth in grace in your major battlefields— alienation, unforgiveness, and bitterness. I bless you to come into alignment with God's purposes, so that there is less struggle between spirit, soul, and body. You are the first-fruits of God's gifts, and I bless you with maturing into God's beautiful full intention. Let him call the expression of your gift up higher into all that he sees when he looks at you. I bless with you with gaining from the Spirit of God a new understanding of who you are as God designed you to be. I bless you in Jesus' name. Amen.

56

Servant

Servants prefer to be invisible and in the background. They work very hard, even hurting their own physical health. Servants find their greatest fulfillment in knowing they are a life-giver who makes it possible for somebody else to do their work. They greatly enjoy helping leaders fulfill the call of God on their life. Servants have a great gift for loving the unlovable, the hard cases. They are "porcupine-huggers." They have special authority when praying for restoration in the family, for the sick, especially in threatened premature death, for nature and weather, and for land issues. Servants battle against the victim mindset and self-worth issues. They tend to tolerate indignity and shaming, especially in their families. They tend to believe lies about themselves that cause them not to feel legitimate or adequate for spiritual responsibilities or positions of authority. They will always tell you someone else is better qualified. Servants have a strong ability to see external needs of comfort and food and are quick to meet those needs. They are team players. Servants are known for being very practical. They are committed to the present moment to meet present needs. They have a heart for preparing the way for others to enjoy the presence of God.

Biblical Examples Of Servant: Ananias (who went to Saul), Barnabas, Esther, Timothy, and Joseph (Mary's husband).

Principle Of Authority

The principle of authority parallels the gift of servant. The specific stronghold that comes from the perversion of the principle of authority is the victim spirit. The root iniquity is embracing peace at any cost. The central virtue is living in dominion. There is a big difference between the words "domination" and "dominion." To dominate somebody means to exercise authority over them in such a way that you take that which is rightfully theirs for yourself. You control them at a loss to them and a gain to you. We are to live in the dominion and authority given to us through Christ (Ephesians 2:6). Dominion is exercising authority in order to bring people into submission to the life-giving laws of God. It involves causing demons as well as nature to submit to God's authority (Luke 16:19). Dominion is always in a life-giving context in partnership with God.

The key to understanding the principle of authority is that its purpose is always to create more authority for the kingdom of God, not for man. God gives us authority so that we can multiply the number of people and the social structures that are expanding the kingdom of God. Jesus said "All authority has been given to me, and I am with you" (Matthew 28:18,20). The ultimate goal is to redeem, detoxify, and sanctify all individuals and institutions to their highest level. The servant has a natural drive to serve those around them, helping others to become all that they were designed to be. God entrusts the gift of servant with this authority because the servant doesn't desire power for his own sake.

Authority Of Servant

- To pray for leaders. To use authority to care for and minister to leaders. To release leaders from the bondage of administrative tasks in the "outer court" so they can meet with God.

- To restore families. To bring family restoration (salvation, deliverance, healing, etc.).

- To love the "hard cases." To reach the difficult ones who are deeply wounded and fearful of the truth.

- Authority over the death spirit, in particular the premature death spirit. Applies to both spiritual and physical death. Authority over overt potential demonic attack to take a person's life (like Esther did when she stood in the gap against the potential extermination of Israel).

- Authority over land or ecology. The servant speaks blessing and anointing to the land and buildings and can call forth ecological restoration.

Birthright Of Servant

- To live in their authority as a life-giver to others, especially to leaders, so the leaders can do the work God called them to do.

- To provide the cleansing and authority others require to reach their destiny.

- To restore broken families, defiled land, and the ecology.

Number Line For The Scale Of Responsibility

+100 The capacity to transform a community. Able to extend authority, peace, secured boundaries, and freedom to a community.

+80 Extending authority in the church. Can function inside imperfect institutions and bring them into more godly authority. The paralysis of the church does not paralyze them. It is more difficult to bring the authority of God to bear on the religious community than on the secular community. The "lawless" ones more readily accepted Jesus than the religious.

+60 Extending authority at work. Greater respect of boundaries at work. Others in the workplace begin living in greater authority.

+40 Discipleship. Bringing others from negative numbers to plus numbers in their lives. Visible fruit from investing in others. Able to provide resources and minister to others.

+20 Growing authority in their own life. Receiving and releasing more of God's peace and authority. More skilled at recognizing positive potential in a situation or person that can be redeemed. A greater understanding of the principles of God's Word and how to use them to resist Satan and heal a broken person. Has secured boundaries for self and others. Experiencing greater freedom from the demonic, seasons between attacks get longer, and temptations get weaker or less frequent.

0 No longer a victim, but not doing anything to expand their authority.

-20 Lacks personal authority. Looks to an institution to give them authority and legitimacy but does not feel they have authority on their own. Authority should be based on our position in Christ, not in an institution. Not living in overt abuse, but lacks victory.

-40 Not tolerating abuse but still trapped in it. Generally life-giving and receiving, but they have an area where they have zero victory. Tend to stay in relationships that are damaging and wounding. They lack the key to their freedom. Do not have authority and are still in bondage in a particular area.

-60 Living in "acceptable" pain and victimization. The level of pain is no longer excruciating, but they have chosen to accept their current level of pain as normal. They accept abuse because -60 feels so much better than -100.

-80 Despairing victims. Aware something is wrong. Able to see what justice, law, integrity, and freedom are supposed to look like but are hopeless and paralyzed. Has no idea how to move forward.

-100 Completely victimized. Abused by men and demons. The victim spirit is so strong that they don't even know they're victimized. There is no sense of anything more than survival.

Moabite Curse

Biblical Basis: Judges 3:12-30

Once again the Israelites did evil in the eyes of the LORD, and because they did this evil the Lord gave Eglon king of Moab power over Israel. Getting the Ammonites and Amalekites to join him, Eglon came and attacked Israel, and they took possession of the City of Palms. The Israelites were subject to Eglon king of Moab for eighteen years. Again the Israelites cried out to the Lord, and he gave them a deliverer—Ehud, a left-handed man, the son of Gera the Benjamite. The Israelites sent him with tribute to Eglon king of Moab. Now Ehud had made a double-edged sword about a foot and a half long, which he strapped to his right thigh under his clothing. He presented the tribute to Eglon king of Moab, who was a very fat man. After Ehud had presented the tribute, he sent on their way the men who had carried it. At the idols near Gilgal he himself turned back and said, "I have a secret message for you, O king. "The king said, "Quiet!" And all his attendants left him. Ehud then approached him while he was sitting alone in the upper room of his summer palace and said, "I have a message from God for you." As the king rose from his seat, Ehud reached with his left hand, drew the sword from his right thigh and plunged it into the king's belly.... v. 29 At that time they struck down about ten thousand Moabites, all vigorous and strong; not a man escaped. That day Moab was made subject to Israel, and the land had peace for eighty years. Verse 13 says the Moabites took possession of Jericho, the City of Palms. Jericho was the major crossing across the Jericho River and was a place of international commerce. The Moabites were controlling how much the Israelites could move around and trade with others. The Moabite curse causes those in authority to limit the freedom of those under them, requiring those in bondage to serve at the expense of possessing their own birthright.

Legitimacy Lie

"I am legitimate when I build a platform of success under others." This is a savior mentality.

Signs Of The Curse

- Authorities are supposed to equip and release others by building a platform of success under you. Unrighteous leadership expects you to build a platform under them, serving their purposes at the expense of your calling.
- Your authorities (boss, pastor, parents) do not equip and release you, either actively by holding you back or passively by ignoring you and not helping you to succeed.
- Money is continuously devoured before it gets to you, or promises are continually broken.
- The key issue is a violation of personal boundaries.

Possible Cause

- You or someone in your family remained passive under bondage because it was "easier" than standing up or leaving.
- You or someone in your family took freedom the wrong way by responding with rebellion or resentment toward those who were in authority, even if they were unrighteous.

Personal boundaries are continually violated in one or more of these areas.

Sexual boundaries

Women have maintained moral purity, and yet every time they get around men, their boundaries are crowded. May be as subtle as a hug that is too long, or a man standing too close, or feeling someone looking at them and undressing them with their eyes without touching them.

Personal space

At work their desk, office space, or items are used without asking. No respect of their own space or things.

Time

Others do not respect their time and expect them to be available 24/7 to meet their needs regardless of their schedule.

Your Reputation

There are normal cultural rules for what to do with private information. Those under the Moabite curse are talked about in inappropriate ways. Example: Someone tells a personal prayer request to two of their closest intercessors. The next Sunday it is discussed at random by people in the church with a total disregard to privacy.

Relationships

There are emotional relationships in which others are demanding things, and it is open-ended. No matter how much they apologize or how much they do, it is never enough. The Israelites had to pay enough money to Moab to keep Moab from hurting them more. But they never knew how much was enough.

- An adult child gets scolded if they forget to call Mom every day. Yet if the child asks Mom, "Do I have to call you everyday from work?" mom will say, "Oh no. I just thought you would love me enough to call me every day." That is guilt manipulation because there is an expectation, and it is denied when confronted. If you fail to make a big enough effort, you are punished for it, but if you try to establish the rules, there is a total denial that the rules exist.

- Family demands a significant amount of your time to be present with them at all holidays, birthdays, and events.

- A child has a gift for drama, but her parents send her to medical school.

- Parents do not want children/grandchildren to move to another city or nation, even if God is calling them there.

- Pastors are unwilling to release people that God is calling to another place. Pastors acknowledge the call of God on the person, but out of selfishness they want that talent and anointing to remain in the church rather than releasing them.

- Boss does not promote someone who is in a job below their talent level, because there is nobody else to put in that position.

61

Prayer Of Renunciation Of The Moabite Curse

Father God, you are the God of seasons. There is a season for nurture and a season to be the nurturer. There is a season for childhood and a season for adulthood. I rejoice in the authority and responsibility that you have given to parents and others in positions of leadership. The proper order of life is for those in authority to build a platform for success for those under their authority and to release them at the proper time.

Open the books in my generational line, and identify every event where an authority figure in my family line or over my family line failed to release those who should have been released. Father, this is contrary to your design. Identify every instance where somebody under authority chose to embrace family peace at the expense of possessing their birthright. That is sin, and I reject and renounce it. Identify every incident where somebody took their freedom wrongly in order to possess their birthright. That is sin. Cover these three classes of sins with the blood of the Lord Jesus Christ.

It was just and right for the Moabite curse to be in my family line because people violated your law, but the righteous law of liberty is greater than the law of sin and death. I stand in the cleansing of the cross of Jesus, and I command every devouring spirit that once was empowered by the sins that are now under the blood to leave me, my spouse, and my physical and spiritual seed to a thousand generations and not to return. Ancient of Days, as the righteous Judge of the universe, enforce your righteous decrees.

Enlarge my boundaries to give me freedom of movement to accomplish everything you have designed for me to accomplish. If I need to leave, give me clear direction about how to do that in a way that you will bless and that will not empower the enemy. In accordance with your Word, release that generational blessing of peace and open borders to my spiritual and physical seed. Thank you by faith in advance in the name of the Lord Jesus Christ, amen.

The Blessing Of Esther

The Moabite Curse causes those in authority to limit the freedom of those under them, requiring those under authority to serve the authority at the expense of possessing their own birthright. Breaking the Moabite curse releases the person to pursue their own life. The blessing of Esther occurs when those in authority over you support and equip you to succeed in your calling. Esther lived in that blessing. When she was orphaned, her relative Mordecai took her in and groomed her for excellence. When she had to face the king, uninvited, for the sake of her life and the lives of the Jews, Mordecai gave her perspective and encouragement and also mobilized all the Jews in the capital city of Susa to fast and pray for three days in support of her mission. That represented a massive community effort to empower her during a critical transition in her reign. It built a platform under her for success. After the initial crisis, the king gave her the authority to govern, but she had no experience in governing. Mordecai came alongside her again with administrative skills which made her look good in the use of the power she had been granted.

Signs Of The Blessing Of Esther

- Secure boundaries and the freedom to expand as God directs.

- Tangible resources flow to you. People who have no responsibility to you do something for you, giving support that enables you to do what God has called you to do.

- People find great fulfillment in building platforms under you. Others want to make you better at what you do. They don't owe it to you; they just choose to do it.

How To Develop In The Blessing Of Esther

- Stop looking for the answer to "Why me?" and begin to focus on God's provision in spite of wounding. Where did God build a platform under you when people didn't? Keep a record of the ways that God has provided for you where your parents did not. Do not default into bitterness. Build a fortress in your life of how God has provided for you. Choose to see his platform under you. God is infinitely larger than any wounding that happened in your life.

- Most people are used to "making do" rather than believing that there should be a system of people and resources in place that God uses to help them succeed. If God gave you something that would enable you to be more life-giving than you are now, what would you ask for? Clearly identify what would enable you to build the kingdom. What are you lacking in order to be equipped and released into what God designed you to be and do?

- Be a tangible life-giving blessing of Esther to someone else you are not responsible for, overtly building a platform under them in material and sacrificial ways, whether you are receiving support or not. Think of a few people and how you can build a platform under them.

Sevens In Scripture

Creation

On the second day of creation, God separated the waters above from the waters below. The waters and atmosphere are pictures of the servant. The atmosphere and water are essential to sustaining life. The atmosphere in most cases is invisible. The primary function of air and water is cleansing impurities and diluting toxins. A servant likewise is frequently invisible or has a low profile. The servant does not like the spotlight and is rarely given it. The term *servant* carries negative connotations in our culture, but that's not how God sees the servant. The servant is not less significant or less vital than the other gifts. Oxygen is the most crucial component for sustaining life. Before God created any other form of life, the atmosphere had to be in place to sustain life. The servant carries an important task of sustaining life through giving spiritual oxygen and through cleansing. A servant can walk through areas of defilement and iniquity without getting personally defiled.

Items Of Furniture In The Tabernacle

The second item of furniture was the bronze laver that provided water for the sacrifices and water to wash the priests (Exodus 29:4; 30:17-21; 38:8). When a priest went from the brazen altar into the holy place, he had to go past the bronze laver and wash himself before he went into the presence of God. This is a picture of the value and the importance of the servant's role. The servant is designed to pray for leaders that they will be cleansed and renewed and will enter into God's presence. The servant is entrusted by God to facilitate the transition from the trenches into the throne room.

Compound Names Of Jehovah

The name of God that parallels the gift of servant is Jehovah-Rapha, "The Lord who heals" (Exodus 15:26). This name of God was spoken when the entire nation of Israel had come out of Egypt. It refers to keeping people whole, preventing disease from coming on them. According to Psalm 105:37, they came out whole and healed. There was none feeble among the tribes. The Lord promised that if they listened to the voice of God, lived righteously, and kept his commands and statues, he would keep them whole. Obedience and a desire to submit to God's authority comes naturally to the servant. God rewards their obedience with wholeness.

Seven Last Sayings On The Cross

Jesus said to the thief, "Today you will be with me in paradise" (Luke 23:43). It appeared that Jesus had nothing to give on the cross, but he knew he was still the Son of God. He had no evidence in the natural to prove it, but in effect he said to the thief, "I am the Savior of the world. My death will provide salvation for the human race. You will be with me eternally." Just like Jesus, servants must come into agreement with who God says they are, regardless of circumstances or appearances or what people around them think they are. The servant's calling is to agree with how God sees them and live in their God-given authority.

Seven Letters To The Churches In Revelation

The redemptive gift of servant parallels the church of Smyrna in Revelation 2:8-11 NKJV.

"I know your works, your tribulation, and your poverty..."

Works: Many things a servant does are not honored by others, but the Father sees them all. He knows intimately the value of all that the servant does.

Tribulation: The servant can be put in a tight place and continue to function. Others often place significant expectations, demands, and pressure on servants. The servant pleases and honors God when they thrive in the midst of tribulation.

Poverty: The servant can appear impoverished by their circumstances, but they are rich in spiritual authority.

"and I will give you the crown of life... He who overcomes will not be hurt at all by the second death." Because of their faithfulness, this church received a double promise: the crown of life and not being hurt by the second death. God trusts the servant to carry high authority (the crown of life) because they will use it for kingdom purposes. The servant carries burdens in prayer for the hard cases and "impossible" salvations. Other gifts don't share these passions with the same intensity. The servant has authority over premature death and the death spirit.

Blessing Prayer For Servant

I bless you for the richness you bring to life in caring for the needs of others in practical ways. You know the blessedness of giving of yourself in acts of kindness, thoughtfulness, and "second-mile" effort for others. You preach sermons without words, with sermons of service.

You have few enemies. I bless your way of love and grace that puts people at ease. You communicate that the purpose of life is people. You are a good listener. You are genuine and personal in relationships. You see the best in others.

I bless your desire to invest your life daily, moment by moment, in things that last. But because of your desire to meet needs and please people, you have difficulty saying "no" to competing demands. You can get overcommitted when you default to meeting people's needs without asking God. I bless you with learning the art of knowing when to serve. God wants to define who you are and help you empower others with responsibility, not enable them. Be free in the Spirit to say a holy righteous "no," even to some good things, in order to say "yes" to God's best.

I bless you for being totally trustworthy and working very hard. You exemplify a life well-lived. Nothing higher can be said than that you love, live for, and give yourself to the right things.

Your strong sense of responsibility tends to attract people who hold their rights and a sense of entitlement. You tend to be exploited by those looking for an enabler. Calling others to grow in character is more important than meeting their immediate needs. I bless you to present your entire being available to God for his purposes, not the agenda of others.

Satan's only defense against the authority and anointing of your servant gift is to get you to believe the lie that you are nobody. Therefore, you tend to have a battle for self-worth. You may have attracted dishonor, especially in the home. I bless you to see the value in yourself and believe God's truth about yourself and your call. Let Jesus impart to your spirit true statements about the honor you are due. I bless you with a download from God of personal identity, worth, dignity, and legitimacy that conquers shame, dishonor, and victimization. I bless you with knowing the honor you have as one who carries the name of Jesus. Your shield of honor is the cross of Jesus. Receive the affirmation of others without finding something to apologize for. Choose to be seen as competent and excellent as you are. God wants people to see who you are as a reflection of his Son Jesus. You are you, and you are beautiful. I bless you to live in humility and love, rejecting dishonor and receiving the honor that Jesus thinks is due you.

I bless you because you see the best in others when no one else does. You minister to the hardest cases, the ones everybody else gives up on. You treat everybody as if you are entertaining angels unawares. You see in a person, whom others have discarded, the potential for that person to be transformed by God and to be life-giving in their world. You embrace the deeply wounded through their pain. You demonstrate that God is a God of second chances.

I bless the purity of your motives. You can be trusted and are straight-forward, possessing integrity, truthfulness, and honesty. I honor you for your qualities of purity of heart.

I bless your loyalty to your family. I bless you with God's purpose, desire, and focus as you minister to them. Ask him to shine his truth on their true needs and your place in meeting them. I bless you to have the mind of Christ and healthy boundaries to provide a safe place for people to find their birthright without rescuing them or falling into a savior mentality. I bless your passion for family and family restoration, for marriage and parent/child relationships. You have authority in prayer to bring the extended family to restoration. Rise up into new authority for specific restoration in people and generational restoration in families—salvation, deliverance, wholeness.

I bless your anointing to bring people back to joy, but you can become a burden-bearer with worry, anxiety, and false responsibility if you take on other people's problems. You are a joy-giver, but you are not responsible for the happiness of others.

You are a team player who likes clear parameters and guidelines. I bless your lack of desire to build your own kingdom. You work well with others. You are jealous for God's honor, and your heart motive is to advance the kingdom of God regardless of the expense to self. It is right for you to not prefer the spotlight. You don't pursue fame or steal God's glory, but ask God to remove from you the label of invisibility. You are irreplaceable and vital to the life of all the gifts and in the body of Christ and the world.

Many leaders have servants around them. You are drawn to leaders and those in authority. You desire to make them successful. You have authority to pray for leaders in all areas. You have great fulfillment in knowing you are a life-giver to those you serve. You desire to empower others to achieve their best. You have a long history of building a platform under others. You have great spiritual authority in prayer to pray for most of the authority structures that God established — marriage, parenting, church, government, and business. God uses your desire for invisibility positively and lets you go into many places under the radar for his prayer assignments.

You are drawn to pray for government. I bless your anointing to pray for governmental authority. When you live in your authority and pray for the life of God to flow into government, God intends that you see measurable results in transformation on spiritual and social issues.

I bless your desire to pray for life-and-death situations. You are tenacious in not accepting death as the answer. I bless your authority to pray especially about premature death, in leaders, family, captives, and wounded ones.

You have a particular stewardship in prayer for healing the ecology and cleansing land, air, and water. I bless your authority for the restoration of the environment that has been damaged by the sin of man. You recognize defilement in land and apply the laws of repentance and cleansing. You intuitively bless land in alignment with the purposes of God in creation. Be bold in prayer to put a heavenly stamp on God's purposes in the earth.

I bless you with being mighty in spirit with wisdom, gentleness, and dignity. I affirm your resilience of spirit as your spirit partners with the Holy Spirit for victory and secure boundaries to operate in peace. Your focal point is God's kingdom of righteousness, peace, and joy in the Holy Spirit. I bless you with quietness and stillness inside and total assurance.

I bless you with seeing more reconciliation, more deliverance, healing, and miracles — signs of God's favor and presence on you, as you move with him in the power of purity in the purifying mantle of the servant. Your glorious release has begun by God's goodness and unmerited grace. I bless you in Jesus' name. Amen.

Teacher

The teacher's need to validate truth is central to their motivation. They are great monitor/ evaluators. They are designed to produce teaching of truth that will carry on for successive generations, but their knowledge must not be academic only. It must also reveal the presence of God in experience. Teachers are very safe people emotionally and can be confused with mercy because they are patient with those who are in sin. The teacher tends to be more in their head, and the mercy is more in their heart. Teachers are willing to lay out the whole picture and allow the other person to choose to do what is right and be reconciled. It is hard for them to compel others to take responsibility. Teachers tend to have selective responsibility. This can lead to things at home getting neglected. Teachers usually have a wonderful sense of humor. They want to see the end before beginning a process, which can cause them to study things endlessly and make decisions slowly. They are a good balance to the more impulsive gifts. They have a deep commitment to family and tradition.

Biblical Examples Of Teacher: Ezra, Isaiah, Luke, Mary (mother of Jesus) and Samuel.

Principle Of Responsibility

The redemptive gift of teacher parallels the principle of responsibility. The demonic stronghold is a religious spirit. The root iniquity that supports the religious spirit stronghold is selective responsibility. The central virtue is effectively sanctifying one's family. The teacher struggles with selective responsibility in his walk with God and in his relationships with others. There is a tendency for the teacher to embrace sin in one area while at the same time passionately pursuing truth in others. The teacher has a strong need to appear to be lined up with truth. The carnal teacher obsesses about religious activity in place of taking social responsibility (for example, the religious establishment of Jesus' day who passed by the injured man while the Good Samaritan stopped to help). God rejects religious activity, no matter how intense, if the teacher is not responsible in dealing with the injustice around him (Isaiah 1:11-17). God calls the righteous teacher to embrace the full principle of responsibility by living out both the first and the second commandment to fulfill their responsibility to God as well as to their fellow man.

Social responsibility is a lifestyle of seeing the needs around you. No one can meet all the needs in their society, but most can meet more than they are meeting now. It is a mindset of being life-giving to others and the community when nobody has told you to, and nobody is requiring it of you. The teacher is designed to use principles in order to solve difficult problems around them, thus taking responsibility for others.

Authority Of Teacher

- Authority to bring blessing, especially generational blessings.

- Authority to call forth life from seed (redemptive death).

- Highest authority over the predator spirit.

Birthright Of Teacher

- To know God's deep truths that can only come through intimacy.

- To know God experientially and to incrementally dispense what God reveals.

- To reveal the manifest presence of God to others by knowing who God is and to live in God's will, to reveal the presence of God to the world and enthrone the Lord Jesus Christ.

Number Line For Scale Of Responsibility For Teacher

+100   **True worship.** In Spirit and truth. Loves the Lord with all their heart and soul and mind. Enjoys the presence of God without all the religious trappings, just as Adam and Eve did.

+80   **Help the unwilling to posses their birthright.** Highly skilled at ministering to those who don't want it, don't ask for it, and don't see the need of it. Many stay at the +40 or +60 level because it is easier.

+60   **Help others to possess their birthright.** Requires more maturity and skill because one should not directly control others. Must trust the Holy Spirit with others for success. It is easier and more gratifying to do it yourself. With freedom comes responsibility.

+40   **Possessing your birthright.** Knows his calling and lives in it. No one can possess his own birthright without learning to be life-giving to the community. Does not seek comfort but fulfillment. Requires being fiercely intentional to develop, sharpen, and use skills.

+20   **Being a life-giver to others.** Embraces the concept of community and social responsibility. Demonstrates community daily in small ways, preferring one another in love. Makes a lifestyle of meeting needs around him. Doing what is good voluntarily, such as returning the shopping cart to the cart enclosure, not littering, picking up the litter of others, returning the pen he walked out of the bank with, etc.

0   **Obedience.** Takes personal responsibility in own life, but does not do more than is expected or required (Luke 17:7-10).

-20   **Selective responsibility.** Takes responsibility in some areas but ignores others. Can tend to be "takers" more than givers in selective areas. Believes "I've done my part, I don't have to do anything else."

-40   **Welfare spirit.** Doesn't own problems. Blames others and expects others to take care of problems for them.

-60   **Forced obedience.** Only obeys the law and God when forced. Not God-seekers. Regularly violates social norms, such as traffic laws. Cheats on income tax, cheats on spouse, commits "victimless" crimes. Can't be trusted to do the right thing when no one is looking.

-80   **Sociopath.** Habitual career criminal, in and out of prison. Takes no social responsibility, regardless of consequences.

-100   **Satan worship.** Satanism, Luciferianism, the occult, Freemasonry.

Philistine Curse

Biblical Basis: 1 Samuel 13:19-22

Not a blacksmith could be found in the whole land of Israel, because the Philistines had said, "Otherwise the Hebrews will make swords or spears!" So all Israel went down to the Philistines to have their plowshares, mattocks, axes and sickles sharpened. The price was two thirds of a shekel for sharpening plowshares and mattocks, and a third of a shekel for sharpening forks and axes and for repointing goads. So on the day of the battle not a soldier with Saul and Jonathan had a sword or spear in his hand; only Saul and his son Jonathan had them.

Genesis 26:12-15

Isaac planted crops in that land and the same year reaped a hundredfold, because the Lord blessed him. The man became rich, and his wealth continued to grow until he became very wealthy. He had so many flocks and herds and servants that the Philistines envied him. So all the wells that his father's servants had dug in the time of his father Abraham, the Philistines stopped up, filling them with earth.

The Philistine curse causes a person to be one piece short of being able to complete a project. In Samuel 13 the shortage was blacksmiths to make weapons. In Genesis 26 it was water. Usually that piece is knowledge or a knowledge-based credential. When you are under the curse, it is very easy for the devil to block your progress. God never used ordinary means to defeat the Philistines. There were ordinary battles for other foes, but when God's people went up against the Philistines at his command, he always gave supernatural strategies.

Legitimacy Lie

"I know the truth, and it gives me power. I am legitimate when I have complete and accurate information. I am legitimate when I am right or have knowledge."

Signs Of The Curse

- You lack key resources to possess your birthright. You seem to have a lot going for you, but you lack one thing or another.
- You cannot put together the package of success that God has called you to.
- You cannot earn what you are worth.

Possible Cause

You or someone in your family used truth in a way that limited and controlled others instead of equipping and empowering them. It can come in two ways.

- Enslaving others with truth. For example, wrong teaching on gender issues to keep women improperly submissive.
- Manipulatively withholding truth or telling partial truth in order to control others and keep them dependent on you. The motivation is to build your own kingdom, where others look to you as the source of knowledge rather than looking to God.

Prayer Of Renunciation Of The Philistine Curse

Almighty God and heavenly Father, the earth is yours. You created it, and you designed it to be under your dominion. You called man to live in dominion and to keep the earth under the kingship of Jesus Christ. I confess that I and my family have failed miserably. We have enthroned the enemy on your land and in our lives. I reject and renounce the sins that opened the door for the Philistine curse. I reject the fear of man that has caused me and some of my forefathers to not obey truth because of fear of offending someone. I confess this as iniquity, and I repudiate that cowardice. I and some of my forefathers have used knowledge of truth as a basis for personal legitimacy. That is iniquity. I and some of my forefathers have used truth to bring people into bondage. I have attempted to control through truth. That is wrong. The truth was designed to set people free. It is not to be used to bring people into bondage to human institutions.

Open the books at every point in my family line where this iniquity has come in. It was just and right for the Philistine curse to come into my family line because of these iniquities. I appeal to the greater source of justice and righteousness, the death of the Lord Jesus Christ and his finished work on the cross, which is more than enough to blot out every sin and iniquity my forefathers committed. Apply the blood of Christ to blot out these iniquities. Based on the word of my testimony, the blood of the Lamb and the promises in your Word, I appropriate cleansing now. I command every demonic structure that has been established in my life or my ministry to be torn down, in the name of Jesus. I command this blocking, devouring spirit to leave my family, my physical and spiritual seed to a thousand generations. Consume with your fire all evil dominion that enthroning the enemy has left in our family line. Restore the years that the locusts have eaten. Restore the blessings that should have been mine that were robbed from me because of this curse. Especially restore godly covenant relationships so that I can be a person of destiny. Teach me how to live in the opposite spirit. Give me your strategies for possessing the land, for possessing my birthright and the resources needed to accomplish your will.

You alone know what is necessary in my life. Speak the truth, and give me the grace to live out that truth no matter how strange it appears. You are welcome in my life. I transfer ownership of all that I am and all that I have to Jesus Christ. I bend my knee and proclaim him King over my life. I do this in the presence of earthly witnesses, the angelic realms, and the demons themselves. Lord Jesus Christ, release your godly dominion over all that I am and all that I have. Amen.

Blessing Of Daniel

The blessing of Daniel is receiving from God supernatural strategy to overcome the opposition of the enemy, instead of having to war vigorously for each victory. You overcome the devil with greater ease than the ease with which he stopped you in the past. God never used ordinary means to defeat the Philistines. He always gave supernatural strategies to his people when they went up against the Philistines at his command. Shamgar, son of Anath, struck down six hundred Philistines with an oxgoad (Judges 3:31). Samson caught three hundred foxes and tied them tail-to-tail in pairs. He then fastened a torch to every pair of tails, lit the torches, and let the foxes loose in the standing grain of the Philistines to destroy their crops (Judges 15:4-5). Samson killed a thousand men with the jawbone of a donkey (Judges 15:14-15). David killed Goliath the Philistine with a slingshot (1 Samuel 17).

Daniel refused to engage in a normal, legitimate power play. Serving as the top-level officer in a great kingdom, he refused to embrace human power as a means of defeating evil. Each of his victories stemmed from an uncommon strategy and required minimal effort on his part. Each of his victories had far-reaching effects, bringing life to many more than just those involved in the events themselves. The blessing of Daniel allows you to overcome the devil swiftly, rather than being delayed in life with an extended, grinding spiritual battle.

Signs Of The Blessing Of Daniel

- God gives you unique revelation (intellectual capital) that you need to progress.

- The Lord Jesus Christ is enthroned in your life and on the land. The presence of the enthroned Lord keeps many devourers away.

How To Develop In The Blessing Of Daniel

- Celebrate how God has shown others truth that has set you free instead of controlling you.

- Celebrate times when God sent you wisdom in a package you didn't like or appreciate in order to set you free. You didn't enjoy the pain at the time, but later you used it as wisdom.

- Be willing to embrace new problems to find new revelation about who God is and the truth he desires you to know. God gives us problems to teach us many things. Most parents do not do that for their kids. They are constantly trying to create a problem-free and pain-free environment. Our response to a problem is often, "I will never solve this problem," but God does not bring problems that we will never be able to solve. The correct response to a problem is, "I may not know how to solve this problem now, but I have the ability to solve this problem within me." Are you doing something today that you could not have imagined doing ten years ago? Have you ever said, "If God had told me everything about his plan for me from the beginning, I would have said it was impossible"? When you embrace problems and situations that don't have easy answers, God brings new truth and revelation to you.

- Minister to people whom God sends you even if their problems are outside your area of expertise. Has God sent you a person whom you have chosen not to minister to because you don't feel you know how? Success can be the greatest barrier. People tend to become "specialists," ministering only to those they know they can be successful with, because they are afraid of not performing well or losing their reputation. See others for who they are. Focus on what they have to give to the community, instead of what they can't do when compared to others. In other words, help them develop their God-given strengths rather than focus on their weaknesses.

When we come up against things that don't have easy answers, the core issue is knowing the Father heart of God. Can you trust him to come through for you when there are no easy answers? Or do you only choose to engage in that which is safe and easily resolved?

Sevens In Scripture

Creation

The third day of creation parallels the gift of teacher. On the third day of creation God separated the sea from the dry land. He planted trees and herbs and seed-bearing plants. Plants draw nutrients from the soil and convert them into wood, food, and herbs for nourishment and healing. The seed uses the inert life in the land and converts it to a useable form. That is the role of the teacher. The seed that the teacher works with is truth. As the teacher deals with people, they may seem as inert as a piece of land. They may not seem to have life, but as the teacher brings truth to bear, the miracle of growth begins to take place and out of their life flows life that was not there before. Every human being carries potential. They are made in the image of God. In 2 Peter 1, there are eight virtues of the Christian life. If you have these things in increasing measure, you will not be ineffective and unproductive in your knowledge of God. It is the teacher's job to make them effective and productive. The teacher has the truth and the ability to produce that conversion, to take the unfruitfulness of their life and bring the precise truth at the precise moment to bear in that inert soil. God has placed a hunger for truth in the teacher that can never be completely satisfied. The teacher's design is to work diligently at seeking out truth, verifying, sorting out good seed from dead seed. Like trees and plants that bear fruit for many seasons, the teacher will produce fruit that will multiply for generations. The teacher's passion should be to take truth and sow it lavishly in the soil of the lives they meet.

Items Of Furniture In The Tabernacle

The third item of furniture in the tabernacle was the table of showbread or the bread of presence (Exodus 35:23-30; 37:10-16). The elements of this table reveal part of the design and calling of the teacher. On the table there was frankincense and twelve loaves of bread. At the end of the week the priests ate the old bread and placed twelve fresh loaves of bread before Lord. Jesus is the bread of life. The frankincense is a symbol of worship. The number twelve symbolizes the tribes of Israel, God's government manifested here on earth. Only the priest were allowed to eat the holy bread, revealing something about the level of intimacy they shared with God. The teacher is designed for intimacy with Jesus, the Bread of life, the Word incarnate, the one who reigns as King over all earthly governments and the one who is worthy of worship. The teacher is gifted at digging in the Word and seeing new facets of the presence, nature, and dominion of Jesus Christ. As the teacher sees the unfolding of Jesus in the Word, he responds with worship. Worship is a response to discovery of truth about who God is. The ultimate goal of truth is not knowledge, but to celebrate the kingship of Christ in worship. This is a battlefield for the teacher in the way he studies the Word of God. His ultimate goal must be intimacy and worship, not simply accumulating doctrine and knowledge.

Compound Names of Jehovah

The third of the seven compound names is Jehovah-Nissi, "The Lord our Banner" (Exodus 17:8-16). Verse 15 says "Moses built an altar and called it The Lord is my Banner." He said, "The LORD will be at war against the Amalekites from generation to generation." The Israelites had been slaves in Egypt and had developed a victim mentality. Although they were free, they still felt like slaves. In Exodus 14 when Moses and the people of Israel were at the Red Sea, the Lord said to them, "Why are you crying out to me?" God told Moses to use his staff and for the people of Israel to move forward. At the battle in Exodus 17, for the first time Moses and the Israelites lived as sons by using what they had learned at the Red Sea, instead of crying out in despair to God again. They applied principles to a new problem and lived in sonship. In Exodus 17:14, God instructed Moses to write all of the events on a scroll for Joshua. The teacher extends principles from one problem to another and from one person to another. God makes a generational promise to Israel of protection against their predators, the Amalekites. The teacher has an anointing to overcome the predator spirit.

Seven Last Sayings On The Cross

Each one of the seven sayings parallels a challenge for that redemptive gift. In the third saying of Christ on the cross, he spoke to his mother and his disciple John. "Behold your son, and behold your mother." He established a new relationship between them. The principle for the teacher is responsibility, and the challenge for the teacher is imposing responsibility on others. Many teachers are highly responsible in their own realm, but it is a challenge for them to impose responsibility. Yet it is necessary for the teacher to appropriately impose responsibility for certain things. Jesus entrusted the responsibility of his mother to John. He fulfilled his responsibility to care for his mother, and he added responsibility to John to care for her. The natural tendency of the teacher is to explain, reason, and put forth truth, expecting or hoping the other person will pick up the truth and act on it voluntarily. That is the strength of the teacher— his patience, his willingness to lay out the whole picture, and allow the other person to choose. But many times the person does not step up to the challenge, and the teacher must move out of a passive role and say, "This is what you need to do."

Seven Letters To The Churches In Revelation

The gift of teacher parallels the church of Pergamum in Revelation 2:12-17. *"You remain true to my name. You did not renounce your faith."* God designed the teacher to be deeply committed to the truth of the Word, to theology, and to accurate interpretation of the Word. The teacher is skilled in understanding the details of the Word and is committed to their biblical position. Loose exegesis or poor scholarship grates on the teacher. God made the teacher to be passionate about his Word and about treating it accurately. In this, the teacher reflects the nature of Jesus. Some people may not appreciate the teacher's deep commitment to truth. The conflicts of Jesus with the religious leaders were usually around interpretation of the Scripture. When religious leaders attempted to misuse or warp or pervert the meaning of the Word, Christ always destroyed their arguments. However, in his ministry to the disciples, Jesus did not usually split hairs and argue over things with them.

Designed For Fulfillment

"You have people there who hold to the teaching of Balaam, ...you also have those who hold to the teaching of the Nicolaitans. Repent ..." Like the church of Pergamum, teachers struggle with being responsible in some areas (staying true to God's name) and not taking responsibility in other areas (allowing other beliefs to remain unchecked). Teachers can be too soft on sin and selective in their responsibility.

"I will give some of the hidden manna. I will also give him a white stone with a new name written on it, known only to him who receives it." God has truth that he has released to a limited number of people in a few circumstances that is not available to the general populace. When Paul returned from heaven, he said he saw things that were not lawful to utter here on earth. God shared some things with Daniel and with John and told them not to share them. The teacher knows there is more truth to be discovered about God. There is a God-designed craving in the teacher, yearning to find deeper knowledge and a different kind of knowledge, a different wisdom, the hidden manna. The second promise is the white stone with a new name written on it, known only to him who receives it. A name is a form of legitimacy, a tool that communicates connectedness and position and where you are in the social structure. The gift of teacher has a drive to know who he is and where he fits. That desire will not be completely satisfied in this life. There is a craving for legitimacy that flows from relationship, not accomplishment and knowledge. The name on the white stone will express the teacher's unique relationship and place in God.

Blessing Prayer For Teacher

I bless your God-given need to validate truth. It is central to who you are. You serve the body of Christ when you look at things from a number of different angles to validate truth. This is one of the best ways to identify the teacher gift (Luke 1:1-4). Luke, with his teacher gift, wrote more details on the history of the early church than any other New Testament author.

You have a hunger for understanding that causes you to ask many questions. I bless you to celebrate the power and presence of God, seeing his fingerprints and rejoicing over what he is doing. I bless you to incarnate the person and character of Jesus, not just document him. Resist the temptation to verify truth with your natural wisdom and rely on your knowledge, intellect, or education. I bless you to cultivate relationship with Jesus and see him in the Word, and to know him, not just know about him (John 5:39-40; Jeremiah 9:23).

I honor you for your commitment to go to the Word of God first. The best reflection of God's truth is incarnated in your life, not in discussions or arguments or words or ideas. I bless you to take care of your own spirit, so that you can speak into the emptiness of others and share truth relevantly and persuasively.

I bless your gift that causes you to be careful and precise in sharing details, like Luke. Luke 3:1 is a snapshot of the detailed and historically accurate mindset of a teacher. I bless you to move in the strength of your gift and to mine the goldmine of your gift.

You prefer the old, established, and validated because the tried-and-true is more credible to you. You make others stop and consider things biblically. You are not easily swayed from the truth, an anchor against every wind of doctrine. We need your anchor to the Word to not spin off after every religious fad. We need you to systematically organize and present truth, yet make going forward in God the point of reference for all choices, not defending what was. I bless you with a new word in your vocabulary… yet. We've never done it that way… yet.

Some teachers look for more credentials or more degrees to attest to their competence. This is man's validation and legitimizing. Identity is the issue. When that is settled in Christ, you understand who you are, and you know your purpose. Then you can step up into leadership without further validation from man. I bless you with hearing and knowing who you are and what your Father designed you to do.

You process and make decisions slowly. In your search for truth, find the true wisdom of trusting God when you can't figure things out. One of your strengths is that you do not reject new ideas outright, but you do not go forward as quickly as visionaries think you ought to. Repeatedly Scripture says of Mary, "She pondered all these things in her heart." Give your spirit the space, the time, and the solitude it needs.

I bless the way God designed you. God made you the way you are, and he likes you the way you are. God did not make a mistake when he designed you. You listen, observe, gather all

79

Designed For Fulfillment

the evidence, process everything, and summarize it in your mind. Then you give one or two sentences that summarizes and clarifies the whole picture. God made you to slow down impulsive people who jump to conclusions too quickly. The synergy of the prophet, teacher, and mercy can be huge when you work together bringing your strengths to bear. Prophet presents truth and brings to conviction, teacher is ready to point the way back to reconciliation, and mercy brings healing and cleansing into alignment.

I bless you as God challenges your faith, when you want to know the outcome before beginning. You may not be willing to begin a process until you can see the end. God gives the next step, and he expects you to obey that before he reveals what comes next. I bless you to not let fear immobilize you and keep you from obeying God.

You are deeply committed to leadership. Samuel's loyalty to Saul exemplifies this. God removed Saul and his family line from his position as king because of his iniquity, yet Samuel grieved for him. Likewise Luke was loyal to Paul to the end when Demos, Crescens, Titus, and others went off in different directions. I bless your deep loyalty to leaders.

You tend to have a wonderful sense of humor and can defuse a volatile discussion with a quick, charming one-liner. You are a safe person emotionally, and wounded people feel comfortable being around you. You can listen to brokenness and sin without a critical attitude. You will not reject a person in sin and will lay out a path of obedience for him and let him choose. You are great at holding the standard of righteousness and making the way of reconciliation after there has been a violation of the standard. Isaiah modeled this in Isaiah 1:1-15. This is classic teacher. I bless your priestly strength and calling of presenting people to God and representing God to people with blessing.

Intimacy and prayer can be a battleground for you. Pursue intimacy with God at the very highest level. Don't settle for knowledge and miss intimacy with God in in-depth personal interaction with him. You have the duality of validating truth and experiencing intimate relationship with him. Live in intimacy and worship by feeding both your spirit and your mind. Cultivate listening to both the Word and the Spirit speaking to you and encouraging you, the best of both worlds— spirit and truth.

I bless you, teacher, to reveal Jesus as he is. I bless you to come forth with righteousness, refreshment, refuge, redemption, restoration, reconciliation, and resurrection. This is your time to show the world the Lord Jesus Christ who reveals the Father, to have that kind of intimate personal relationship.

Responsibility is the key issue for the teacher. You tend to be unwilling to impose responsibility on others and have difficulty compelling others to do what is right. You do not like to take the initiative to confront that which is wrong. You wait for the sinner to become convicted and come for help. This is a strength, and it can be a weakness if you are too tolerant of sin, too patient with people who are doing wrong. It is appropriate to give people time to repent.

We thank God for your gift. There is a time for showing kindness, but there is a time for confronting. When God says, "Enough!" I bless you with sensitivity to his voice. I bless you to be filled with wisdom, understanding, counsel, knowledge, fear of the Lord, and wise God-centered confrontation when necessary in the right time.

I bless you in areas where you excel in responsibility, and I bless you to not to compartmentalize responsibility. I bless your responsibility and stewardship across the board which the Father has entrusted to you, particularly at home. I bless you to develop the discipline necessary to support your giftedness.

I bless you to be a son, not a slave. I bless your sons to be taught of the Lord, and great will be their peace. I bless you to fulfill your gifting in your generation so that life and healing are released for succeeding generations. I bless your generational nurturing of your sons and daughters—physical and spiritual—in the training and reverence of the Lord, so that generational blessings will pursue subsequent generations.

I bless this time of your birthright with all the timeliness of Ecclesiastes 3:1-11. I ask God to give you significant authority in the blessing of Daniel, where you have the information that you need in a timely manner for strategic options, as you are committed to using the truth to set people free. Prepare the way of the Lord in righteous alignment with his purposes and his time. I bless you with great anticipation, great joy, great peace, great hope and great fulfillment in Jesus' name. Amen.

Exhorter

The exhorter is called to a public ministry to help others see God in practical ways and to mobilize large numbers of people to act. The strength of exhorters is their ability to build relationships. Where there has been disunity or division, the exhorter has a high anointing to restore harmony and reconciliation in a situation. Time is the battlefield of the exhorter. Exhorters are always doing more, always very busy. Exhorters tend to get sucked into the tyranny of the urgent. They are driven by relationships and new opportunities. Exhorters must control their time to "go vertical" with God to know him so they can show him to others horizontally. They may settle for the good and popular, instead of God's best. Exhorters are very sensitive to rejection or criticism from within the group. Exhorters must be willing to risk offense to obey God. Exhorters don't readily confront sin. They tend to take the less confrontational path. Many have others around them who will cover for denial, lack of responsibility, poor judgment, or immaturity. God demands holiness in their character because their calling is great. The birthright of the exhorter is to know God and to reveal him to others. They are excellent communicators of God's Word and his character and find profound fulfillment in knowing God and revealing him to others.

Biblical Examples Of Exhorter: Moses and Paul.

Principle Of Sowing And Reaping

In order to possess their birthright, exhorters must master the principle of sowing and reaping. The cult of comfort is the opposing stronghold which puts immediate pleasure ahead of the long-term and seeks to reap where it has not sown. Denial is the root iniquity that supports and empowers the stronghold of the cult of comfort. Consequently, the central virtue is incarnating wisdom. The principle of sowing and reaping means using God's principles to produce long-term, cumulative life change, not just an immediate change or the illusion of change. Sowing and reaping is focused on the long-term. Ideally, it is focused on corporate activity, although it does apply to individuals as well. It is easy for the exhorter to win the trust of people. His greatest skill is his ability to finesse relationships. God designs exhorters to use these skills to connect them to God and expand his kingdom. Unfortunately, the skill in finessing relationships can so easily cross over the line from that which is good and godly to manipulation. When exhorters become skilled at manipulating, at controlling other people for their own sake, it is very easy for them to move into the habit of avoiding the consequences of their own wrong choices. Denial can keep exhorters from accepting personal responsibilities for their own failures. Immature exhorters can believe they can con, finesse, or manipulate God, but he requires genuine legitimate sowing and reaping according to the principles of natural law and his laws. God designs exhorters to use all of their God-given talent, relationship skills, and personality, combined with godly character, to mobilize large numbers of people who may or may not desire to pursue God's will, to fulfill God's kingdom agenda. Exhorters are at their finest when they commit themselves to long-term sowing in their own personal relationship with God in order to reap a harvest of revelation of relationship with the Father to share with others.

Authority Of Exhorter

- To govern by influence over a large number of people.

- To live in reconciliation with power.

- To very broadly spread the knowledge of God to the world.

Birthright Of Exhorter

- To reveal God to others.

- To know God's will and mobilize large numbers of people to act on his will.

Number Line For Scale Of Responsibility For Exhorter

+100 Fathering. Reveals the Father in social structures as life-giving synergies, causing them to work together instead of competing (civil government, churches, business).

+80 Healing a broken community. Empowers the community through reforming values.

+60 Principle vs. personality-driven change. Leads a community where life and productivity are multiplied through the use of principles, rather the depending on the force of personality or using an event to present a message.

+40 Bring individuals from brokenness to maturity. Involved in mentoring others, not just public speaking. Willing to invest months or years with those they are discipling.

+20 Invest in personal growth. Realizes that character is more important than talent. Willing to invest a significant amount of time in their personal growth. Committed to the Spirit and the Word. The Spirit without the Word can lead to substituting charisma and personality for the Spirit. Must live out the truth, not just teach it.

0 Live in reality. Embraces the pain and cost necessary to achieve excellence.

-20 Denial. Denies the consequences of wrong choices. "Spin-Doctor." Blames the enemy for negative things when often they are reaping what they sowed, financially, relationally, health-wise, etc. It's not all the devil's fault all the time. Also occurs when they claim God's blessing when his manifest presence is not there.

-40 Entitlement. Believes they have the right to receive without having earned it. There are two problems with this system. First, there is no logic to determine who gets the benefits. Second, when they get something they haven't earned enough times, they believe they have a right to it. It becomes an expectation and a demand.

-60 Intentional use of manipulation for personal gain. They use fear to exploit or sell. Dressing for power or seduction. Flattery. Claiming glory for things they haven't done. Claiming people will be blessed if they do what they want them to do or give to their ministry, etc.

-80 Promoters of iniquity. Believes and/or teaches that there are no consequences for iniquity. Believes that sins such as promiscuity, homosexuality, abortion, debt, gluttony, and exploitation of employees have no physical, emotional, social, or spiritual side effects.

-100 Illumination. Seeks world dominion through the skillful, perverted use of natural law, weaving together business, government, and religion into one package to implement the devil's agenda.

85

Canaanite Curse

Biblical Basis: Genesis 9:18-27

The sons of Noah who came out of the ark were Shem, Ham and Japheth. (Ham was the father of Canaan.) These were the three sons of Noah, and from them came the people who were scattered over the earth. Noah, a man of the soil, proceeded to plant a vineyard. When he drank some of its wine, he became drunk and lay uncovered inside his tent. Ham, the father of Canaan, saw his father's nakedness and told his two brothers outside… v. 24 When Noah awoke from his wine and found out what his youngest son had done to him, he said, "Cursed be Canaan! The lowest of slaves will he be to his brothers." He also said, "Blessed be the Lord, the God of Shem! May Canaan be the slave of Shem. May God extend the territory of Japheth; may Japheth live in the tents of Shem, and may Canaan be his slave."

Canaan's sin was that he saw his father naked. He did not cover Noah up but instead went outside to persuade his two brothers to lower their standards as well. Judges states that the Israelites were forced to stay in the hill country and could not go down to the most fertile ground, because the Canaanites were there with their iron chariots. Israel could not fully develop, because they were constantly concerned about the Canaanites who were in the land (Joshua 17:16-18; Judges 1:27-29). The Canaanite curse causes a person to be so overworked by the demands of others that they have no time to develop their own giftings and potential.

Legitimacy Lie

"I am legitimate when people want and need to be around me."

Signs Of The Curse

- You are regularly exploited by leaders. One of the most hurtful aspects of this devouring is that because of exploitive bosses, you don't have the opportunity to develop the God-given abilities within you.
- You are so busy putting out fires and serving someone else that you cannot develop the call of God on your own life.
- There is no time to invest in the future. It is the *Alice In Wonderland* syndrome, running as fast as I can just to stay in place.

Possible Causes

- You or someone in your family used their influence to induce other people to do wrong, frequently in the area of moral impurity.
- Somebody used their influence with those in leadership to lower the standard by either participation or silence on moral matters.
- Someone lowered God's standard for righteousness. They were more concerned about their relationships than the Father's honor.
- Refusing to take responsibility for actions and accept the consequences and reproofs of sin.
- Believing you are entitled to God's blessing without sowing what is required.

86

Prayer Of Renunciation Of The Canaanite Curse

Almighty God and heavenly Father, you are the source of life and the source of authority. In you life and authority meet. You are absolute authority, and yet it is utterly life-giving. I acknowledge that I have not lived in life-giving authority. Open the books of my life and of my forefathers in my family line.

I reject and renounce the belief that legitimacy can be established through popularity. I confess that I and some of my forefathers have lived in that belief. I reject that lie. I reject and renounce the spirit of denial that refuses to recognize the reproofs of life. I reject and renounce shifting the consequences of my bad choices to others. I reject and renounce the perversion of invoking love, loyalty, or submission to force somebody to pay the price for my sin. I reject and renounce the deception of living in supposed love, loyalty, and submission to pay the price for somebody else's sin. I reject and renounce the spirit of entitlement. True sowing is necessary, and there is a proper crop that comes from every seed that is sown.

I reject and renounce embracing visions that require exploitation of the people of God and legitimizing those visions in the name of God. I reject and renounce my sin of using popularity to normalize iniquity, especially moral impurity, and to lower your holy standards. I reject and renounce the sin of staying in an abusive situation to the point that I have not possessed my birthright. It was sin for Israel to be comfortable in the mountains and not exterminate the Canaanites. It is sin to stay in a place that I am not supposed to be for the sake of peace, if it keeps me from possessing my birthright. Bring this cleansing forward through every generation and every branch of my family line. Cleanse me from this iniquity and from the Canaanite curse.

I receive this cleansing. In the name of Jesus of Nazareth, I command every demonic structure and entity that was empowered by those sins and iniquities to leave now and never return. I extend this cleansing and this freedom to my spouse and to my physical and spiritual seed to a thousand generations. Father, give me your strategy, your timing, and your methods to finish exterminating the Canaanite enemies from my life. Teach me how to disengage from entanglements and to move into a place where I have the time and permission to nurture the gifts that you have given me. Teach me and supernaturally aid me. You not only give strategy, but you do miracles. I claim the same measure of victory that Israel had when every Canaanite soldier was killed, including the general. Exterminate every vestige of the Canaanite curse from me, my family line, and future generations. I ask this in the name of Jesus Christ of Nazareth, amen.

Blessing Of Moses

The Canaanite curse causes a person to be so overworked by the demands of their authorities that they have no time to develop their own giftings and potential. When you break the curse, there is discretionary time to pursue unleashing the potential God placed in you. Moses' biggest responsibility was to get to know God and to teach the people of Israel about him. In the wilderness, Moses took control of his own schedule. He had many leaders under him to whom he could delegate, and he had God awaiting him in a tent outside the camp as often as Moses wanted to go visit with him, face-to-face. The fruit of that opportunity to grow was a spirit large enough to write the first five books of the Bible and the authority to appeal to God on world-changing issues. Moses also had the skill to lead a people with a slave mentality. Moses overcame his fear of man in order to try to instill godly principles in a group of people who were prone to grumbling, complaining, and idol worship.

Signs Of The Blessing of Moses

- Time and resources are no longer devoured, but there are time and resources to develop talents and pursue God-given potential. You have enough time to accomplish what you need to accomplish. God trains you in just the right talents. Your resources are always sufficient.

- Those in authority over you encourage you to develop your untapped potential.

- Leaders weave together win-win situations.

How To Develop In The Blessing Of Moses

- Raise the moral bar. As the bar of holiness is raised, others will be drawn to you.

- Challenge wounded people to embrace pain and impose responsibility but do it in the context of compassion for them. Dominion depends on willingness to risk relationship with people for godly principles.

- Renounce being ruled by the fear of man rather than by the fear of God. Celebrate times when you took a risk and stood for truth, risking alienation, and God intervened. Celebrate the goodness of God. People tend to fixate on the intervening enemy, instead of an intervening God. Become God-focused.

- Study biographies of great leaders. Ask two questions: How did they deal with bad people around them? How did they weave together win-win situations in difficult situations?

Sevens In Scripture

Creation

The fourth day of creation parallels the gift of exhorter. On the fourth day of creation God created the sun, the moon, and the stars. He gave them two commands: (1) to mark the day and the night and the seasons of the year and (2) to rule over them. The exhorter is designed by God to have dominion over time and timing, but because of the assault of the enemy, most exhorters do not live in dominion over time. Most exhorters are defeated in time and do not maintain a schedule or arrive on time or start and end on time.

There's a facet of the stars that God created that is not mentioned in the creation story in Genesis. Psalm 19:1-4 says, "The heavens declare the glory of God; the skies proclaim the work of his hands. Day after day they pour forth speech; night after night they display knowledge. There is no speech or language where their voice is not heard. Their voice goes out into all the earth, their words to the end of the world."

Exhorters are known for their wordiness and have been ridiculed, teased, and harassed for their words, but God designed exhorters to be prolific in their use of words to express eloquently and extensively the things that he gives them to express. God created so many stars that it is impossible to number them. All of the stars are saturating the heavens with proclamations and declarations of God's glory. God chose that there should be a torrent of sound pouring forth on the exhorter's day. The exhorter is designed to be verbally expressive, to pour forth speech. But like the stars, the exhorter is designed to speak of God. The weakness of some exhorters is that they speak of small things. God has designed the exhorter to know him and to make him known, to reveal to the world facets of God's nature that are not seen in other ways.

Items Of Furniture In The Tabernacle

The fourth item of furniture in the tabernacle was the golden lamp stand with its oil (Exodus 25:31-40; 37:17-24). The exhorter brings the light of revelation of the nature of God. The light from the golden lamp stand flows from the oil. The oil was to be painstakingly and exquisitely prepared. It was to be clean, pure, and holy with no inferior or defiled oil used to produce the light. This is the exhorter's challenge. The exhorter has a tendency to ignore the line between soul and spirit. Some exhorters will start with a word from God that is a revelation from him. They will begin to reveal light based on their spirit, but because the positive response of people can become addictive, they begin to speak from their soul. The message becomes contaminated with their soulishness. Exhorters must be careful to speak a pure message from pure motives. Exhorters will speak with dominion when they speak in purity, beauty, and strength. God designed exhorters to bring extraordinary light. The exhorter has two strong images of light: the light of the sun, moon, and stars of the creation day and the light of the lamp stand in the tabernacle. No other gift has the light-giving gift of the exhorter. But God wants the light to be pure light, Spirit light not contaminated with soulishness or unholiness.

89

Compound Names Of Jehovah

The fourth of the compound names of Jehovah is Jehovah-Shalom "The Lord our Peace" found in Judges 6:11-24. God revealed himself to Gideon as Jehovah-Shalom at a time when Gideon felt that God has abandoned him and Israel. They were up against a strong enemy and felt defeated. The Lord came to Gideon and showed him that he was with him. The core issue was not Gideon's circumstances, but whether he could trust God to deliver him and Israel. God did not tell him what to do. He only told Gideon to be at peace, because he was with him and he was not going to die. So Gideon built an altar to the Lord there called The Lord is Peace. With this revelation Gideon was able to defeat his enemy. Jehovah-Shalom is not just about peace, but also about the ability to do great things because one has a proper understanding of who God is for us.

Seven Last Sayings On The Cross

Each one of the seven sayings of Jesus from the cross parallels a challenge for that redemptive gift. The fourth saying on the cross was, "My God, my God, why have you forsaken me?" He had already experienced the abandonment of the crowds, the betrayal by Judas, the denial of Peter, and the denial of support and justice from his fellow Israelites in the face of the Roman court, but the crowning blow was a sense of rejection and abandonment by his Father.

On the cross Christ experienced rejection by people and God's abandonment as he turned his face away from his Son for a few hours. All that was left for Jesus was the truth that he knew from God's Word. He had to stand on that alone, unshaken, without any relational connection with God or man at the hour of his most extreme pain.

At times God will allow exhorters to go through rejection and suffer alienation. Exhorters may feel that God is not looking in their direction, that his face is not shining on them anymore. God does that to force exhorters into the position of their greatest and deepest strength. The most obvious and easiest strength of exhorters is relational connection, but their deepest strength is the Word of God. The exhorter has a marvelous ability to get so much out of the Word of God with little effort. The strength of exhorters is to know God, to know his Word, to stand on principle, and to build their life around God's principles. Relationships are the vehicle for the exhorter to deliver the truth of the Word of God. Some exhorters allow the relationships to become primary, just because they are easier. God may strip relationships away to force them into understanding the Word of God that is deeper and greater than the life-flow that is received from relationships. Exhorters must differentiate between the greatest gift and the easiest gift. Horizontal relationships come easily, but the greatest gift is to understand the foundational principles of the Word of God.

Seven Letters To The Churches In Revelation

The redemptive gift of exhorter parallels the church of Thyatira in Revelation 2:19-29. *"I know your deeds, your love and faith..."* The first two elements mentioned of the exhorter's design are love and faith which represents the exhorter's passion for people and for God. Love is the ability to be inclusive of all types of people, even those who are very far from God. Faith is the ability to draw people to God without compromising one's own faith. It is the ability to call people to a higher level of faith in God when they are still far away from God. Exhorters can effectively speak things of faith to pre-Christians.

"...your service and perseverance, and that you are now doing more than you did at first." Most people have an objective, and when that objective is reached, they are satisfied. With exhorters there is a limitless horizon. Although objectives are achieved, the exhorter presses on, seeing more possibilities. Paul did not let prison slow him down. He wrote about the future and the things he wanted to do when he got out. He wrote to the church in Rome about going to Spain. No matter how much exhorters have accomplished or succeeded, they always see more. Others may complain that the exhorter is busy in too many things or taking on more than they can handle, but the DNA of exhorters is to run faster and harder, embracing more to do.

To him who overcomes and does my will to the end, I will give authority over the nations— He will rule them with an iron scepter; he will dash them to pieces like pottery— just as I have received authority from my Father. I will also give him the morning star. Because authority has been corrupted many times throughout history, there is a tendency to consider every craving for authority to be corrupt. But verse 26 says those who overcome will be given authority over nations. The desire to have authority over nations, to judge nations, and to restore nations is an expression of the nature of Jesus. Verse 27 is a quotation taken from a Messianic Psalm. It is a promise that God made to Jesus. Exhorters need to take an honest look at their heart to see if there is any carnal component to their craving. After the flesh and sin are rooted out, bless that which is of God. Exhorters need to look in their heart and see what size leadership God has designed them to have. God desires that they live in that level of dominion and be a world-changer. God intends that the exhorter lead with strength, with divine authority, crushing all opposition and bringing kingdoms into submission to the kingship of Jesus Christ.

Blessing Prayer For Exhorter

God has blessed you with the gift of being a change-agent in your world. You are inspirational and a great motivator who can inspire others to do exploits for God. God designed you to long to put him and his glory on a large stage.

You are fun to be around. You are outgoing, intensely people-oriented and relational. I bless your ability to cross every kind of barrier, socially, racially, economically, and religiously. You can relate to everybody wherever they are and strike up a conversation about heart matters, because you are adaptable, accepted by everybody. I bless your ability to never meet a stranger. You find the key to their heart in a short time. You can relate to the God-shaped vacuum in people. God opens it up to you. I bless you with meeting people where they are and taking them to the next step that God has for them.

I bless your gift for communication. I bless your words, the urgency and frequency with which you speak. God made you to be verbally expressive, and it is good. I bless you to speak of spirit things, life-giving things. You are called to know God and to make him known. I bless you with magnifying the greatness of God. Ask God to give you his voice that is not hindered by the legitimacy needs of the soul. When you have touched God and are sharing him, other people open up their spirits to your spirit to receive revelation about him. I bless you with maturity and growth, being conformed to Jesus that will keep your gift totally spirit-to-spirit.

You are designed to be relational. I bless your ability to light up a room with your presence. You are energized by being with people. You value face-to-face time. You are inclusive. I bless you for bringing others into your circle of influence without compromising your view of God. I bless you for loving God and loving people and wanting to bring the two together. Your relationships are the vehicle for bringing together people with the reality of God. I bless your skill in creating and sustaining relationships. It is one of your most obvious and easiest strengths, but your deepest strength is how quickly you see truth in the Word of God. You can reveal the nature of God and new facets of God to people who already know a lot about him.

You easily transition from small talk to relationship to evangelism. You can speak of faith to a pre-Christian so that he receives it in his spirit when his soul is not interested. You can receive people where they are but challenge them practically, simply, and powerfully to see God bigger. You bring great pleasure to Jesus' heart as you incarnate this portion of himself.

As Jesus listened to his Father, he led his disciples by relationship, persuasion, time, and attention. You are at your finest when you are listening to your Father like Jesus, as you reach, teach, and lead by influence, persuasion, and consensus. You can smoothly bring a group of people to a course of action they need to take. You have a coaching style of leadership.

You are a master of reconciliation over disunity and independent spirits because you can celebrate differences. You are tactful, diplomatic, and approachable. You can smoothly bring a word in an acceptable way. You are an ambassador, a minister, a friend, confidant, listener, affirmer, and counselor. The rest of the body needs your skillset.

92

You are a visionary. You tend to see a broader picture, the largest number of people. You can lay a vision for a diverse group. You are sensitive to the timing and movement of God. You are flexible and quick to see opportunities and change a plan to take advantage of what God is doing at the moment. You are not intimidated by new ideas, new opportunity, new potential, new challenges, or new truth.

Your greatest calling is to know God and to reveal him to others. You are gifted to see God in Scripture. You get so much out of the Word of God with little time and effort. That is an extraordinary gifting from God—to extract nuggets of truths from the Word. I bless you to go vertical with God, hear from him, and discipline yourself to see him in ways others do not, so that you can point out truths others overlook. Jesus revealed his Father in parables, in lessons from life, and you are marvelous at presenting a story. Your teaching style is narrative and illustrative. You speak the message of parable to meet people where they are.

People-pleasing is a battle for everybody at times, depending on our wounding and where we get our significance and legitimacy. I bless you to win the battle of people-pleasing in order to know God and possess your birthright. God forced world-changers Moses and Paul to get to know him in a desert season alone, so they could become mighty in spirit in what he called them to do. In prison God gave Paul revelation that people have benefited from for 2000 years, as he authored the majority of the epistles, the theology, the teaching, and practices of the early church. We are the recipients 2000 years later through his exhorter gift. I bless you with getting God's picture of your God-given abilities of persuasion and leadership and his desire to take you to something that you don't even dream for yourself right now.

I bless you with living by principle and risking reaction, offense, alienation, or rejection for the truth of God without compromise or soft choices. I bless you with the strength of character, wisdom, and grace to confront what needs to be confronted. Paul the exhorter said, "If I were a slave of men, I would not be a slave of God." I bless you with freedom from the need to be liked when God leads you to confront. You will be living in God's highest authority and life-giving anointing when you confront as Jesus did with grace and love. I bless you with placing relationship in its proper place on the altar before God and desiring holiness and obedience to him. The pleasure of the Father is on you when you take the attitude of Jesus toward sin, that it must be dealt with and that he paid the ultimate price to deal with it.

Love and faith and service are markers of the exhorter. You are very busy, function on little sleep, wear many hats, and are involved in many projects. You do an abundance of things and take advantage of many opportunities. That is how God made you. Model your life on how Jesus lived his life. He said, "I have finished all that you have given me to do." Do the work that your Father gives you to do, and don't default into getting your significance from being busy. I bless you to know that your plans are God's plan. Find out where he is at work and join him. Great synergy and great blessing are released, beyond your natural abilities, when you cooperate with God. Often the good is the greatest hindrance to the best. Don't settle for an Ishmael, when God wants to give you an Isaac. I bless you to discover the one thing God wants you to do.

I bless you with taking your God-designed dominion over time and timing. I bless you with not being defeated by time, but having responsibility in time issues. That's who God made you to be. I bless your supernatural design for bringing God's timing and seasons into reality. God designed you to know and to mark the seasons of God because you know the mind of God and you are sensitive to his appropriate timing.

I bless you to know the principle of sowing and reaping. I bless you as you righteously respond to pain and see redemptive lessons in personal pain and suffering. "No pain, no gain." Paul the exhorter wrote one of the most sublime passages in the Bible in Philippians 3:8-10. That is vintage exhorter. You earn authority that comes through embracing personal pain and suffering, so that God releases your authority in his kingdom.

Go to God and get his perspective on the largeness of your calling. I bless you to use the strengths of your skillset: confidence, strength, boldness, and commanding presence in all areas of your God-given authority. I bless you with time, ability, resources, and pathway to develop areas of your greatest potential. I bless your call to reveal God in his greatness, his holiness, his perfection. I bless you to be who God made you to be as a reflection of Christ. Continue to be your joyous, extravagant self. Press hard, run fast, pursue the limitless horizon. I bless you to unleash the Spirit and the Word in the context of community to the glory of God. I bless you to be a reflection of the nature of Christ wherever you go. I bless you in Jesus' name.

Giver

Giver is the most difficult to peg by behavioral characteristics. They are more diverse, adaptable, and flexible. There is much more to this gift than money. A giver can take a concept or idea and bring it to birth because they desire to protect and nurture new ideas. The giver has a generational worldview and a desire to prepare for the next generation. This contrasts with Hezekiah, who did not have a generational worldview. God told Hezekiah that everything he and his fathers had stored up would be carried off to Babylon so that nothing would be left for his descendants and some of them would be slaves in foreign lands. Hezekiah was OK with that because there would be peace and security in his lifetime (Isaiah 39:5-8). God intends givers to be life-givers, releasing generational blessings into their family line, not primarily money. Givers tend to be independent and territorial: what's theirs is theirs. They have ability to find favor with others in terms of money. They are tremendous networkers and have great powers of persuasion. One of the greatest strengths is to get people of different views to work well together toward a goal. They have a need for safety. For givers, everything hinges on their relationship with God. If givers lack holiness and intimacy with God, they will not possess their birthright.

Biblical Examples Of Giver: Abraham, Jacob, Job, and Matthew.

Principle Of Stewardship

The principle of stewardship parallels the gift of giver. The dual strongholds are fear and control. The root iniquity that drives these dual strongholds is ownership, and the central virtue that is needed to overcome them is faith. The ultimate calling of the giver is not just to create changes in his own lifetime, but to extend those changes generationally.

Stewardship is fulfilling someone else's agenda with someone else's resources. There are two common perversions of stewardship. The first is using somebody else's resources to accomplish your own agenda. The other happens often in the religious community as somebody does God's agenda with their own resources, instead of asking God how he wants to provide the resources. The opposite of stewardship is ownership. Ownership is not often thought of as evil. In the United States people pay their taxes, and after they pay their taxes they have ownership of their money. The government does not tell them how to spend the rest of the money. They are free to spend the balance, and that is ownership. However, the New Testament says we are not owners of anything. Everything, including our life, belongs to God. We cannot give God a tithe and spend the rest the way we want to. We are living sacrifices, and everything that we have and everything we are belongs to him. We are to care for it as stewards, as something that belongs to somebody else. We are to use it to accomplish God's agenda. That is very different from ownership. Ownership produces two undesirable fruits: arrogance (using resources for oneself) and fear (holding on to resources for fear one might lose them). Ownership presents the myth that individuals have the right to limit what God does with us and through us. Stewardship says that even our life is in God's hands, and he can take it whenever he wishes. The call of givers is to be a good steward over all that they are given, acting wisely so that the generations to follow may benefit.

Authority Of Giver

- To detect, protect, and bring forth new birth and nurture it.

- Authority to bless generationally.

- Authority to affirm God's design.

Birthright Of Giver

- To release life-giving generational blessings.

- To produce life-giving systems/organizations through holiness and intimacy with God.

Number Line For Scale Of Responsibility For Giver

+100 Generational blessings. Leaving, increasing, and releasing generational blessings for individuals, institutions, communities, regions, and nations. Both Jacob and David did this.

+80 Stewardship over land and nature. God gave to man the command to subdue the natural world. Having proper stewardship of the land and nature for your own community, as well as neighboring communities, through understanding the principles and praying effectively for weather, animals, climate, and land.

+60 Understands the impact of the synergy of the gifts. Two or more of the gifts working together can accomplish more than any gift working alone. For example, the giver does not naturally gravitate toward the gift of prophet, but teaming these two gifts has great potential of being life-giving.

+40 Invests in all three aspects of the family. Spiritual needs, soul-emotional needs, and physical-financial needs.

+20 Is your brother's keeper. Taking care of things that benefit the community, such as shopkeepers who clean the sidewalk in front of their businesses as a public service and act of responsibility.

0 Obedience. Obedient with a vision for God's agenda rather than for own comfort.

-20 Isolation. Basically a good person who doesn't harm anyone else but turns his resources to self-gratification. Life-goal is to protect their own comfort. This is a violation of God's stewardship.

-40 Exploitation of people for personal gain. Misuses social contacts and family to promote personal agenda instead of God's kingdom agenda. Can be sexual exploitation, selling political favors to promote oneself, or being involved in things that may not be illegal, nevertheless exploitive.

-60 Theft. Is also a loss of capital, but instead of destroying the capital, the predator takes the capital and uses it for his own gain. It is more logical than random vandalism or riots.

-80 Destruction of social capital. Loss of resources that a previous generation left behind. For example, riots, vandalism, Sherman's march to the sea.

-100 Bringing generational curses on an entire family, community, or nation. For example, Haiti was dedicated to Satan.

97

Midianite Curse

Biblical Basis: Judges 6:1-6
Again the Israelites did evil in the eyes of the Lord, and for seven years he gave them into the hands of the Midianites. Because the power of Midian was so oppressive, the Israelites prepared shelters for themselves in mountain clefts, caves and strongholds. Whenever the Israelites planted their crops, the Midianites, Amalekites and other eastern peoples invaded the country. They camped on the land and ruined the crops all the way to Gaza and did not spare a living thing for Israel, neither sheep nor cattle nor donkeys. They came up with their livestock and their tents like swarms of locusts. It was impossible to count the men and their camels; they invaded the land to ravage it. Midian so impoverished the Israelites that they cried out to the Lord for help.

The Midianite curse prevents you from accruing the capital needed to produce change through leverage, not labor. The needed resources are generally money and relationships but can include other things. The Midianites would invade every time the crops were ready for harvest and destroy everything. The Midianite curse is a seasonal devouring of capital, such as disease or illness every February or unexpected drain on finances every July, or life falls apart due to physical or financial loss at the same age for everyone in the last three generations. It may be the devouring of family celebrations every year. It can be never being able to get ahead. Just about the time you get out of debt, something breaks, and you have to go back in debt again.

Legitimacy Lie
"I can provide the resources for others to possess their birthright. I am legitimate when I am needed by my family. This can create co-dependency."

Signs Of The Curse
- Things, health, and relationships break or income is lost in a seasonal manner at a particular time or in a pattern.
- Things are devoured for no particular reason.

Possible Cause
- You or somebody in your family line put comfort or security ahead of fulfilling your responsibility and God's calling. You fail to make God's priorities your priority.
- The most common door of entry for this curse is premarital sex or when Freemasonry is used for financial advantage or power. It damages the giver's ability to pursue their birthright.
- The curse comes when you choose comfort over your God-given assignment. Seeking out "magic wand" Christianity where God fixes everything the way you like with no effort on your part versus being willing to embrace the disciplines of the faith.
- Comfort is an idol. It is a series of small steps from social/morally acceptable comfort to comfort that will compromise your birthright. Embezzling God's resources for personal comfort.

Prayer Of Renunciation Of The Midianite Curse

Almighty God and heavenly Father, you are the God of time. Time is the first thing you created on the first day. Therefore, it is the firstfruits of your creation. The first-fruit of everything is dedicated to you, and thereby it is made holy. Since I am a child of God, your intent is that I live in holy time. You do not intend for the seasons of my life to be devoured. I acknowledge that the defilement and the devouring is my fault. Open the books on my family lines and reveal the roots of this curse. I reject and renounce the spirit of control in every branch of my family lines. I repudiate the faithlessness that kept some of my forefathers from possessing their birthright.

I reject the god of comfort and security, and I say that you are able to give tremendous comfort to your people when they possess their birthright. I confess, reject, and renounce the deception from the enemy that it is right for me to postpone possessing my birthright until a more convenient time.

I reject and renounce running ahead of your time and behind your time. Cleanse my generational lines of these iniquities. Remove the Midianite curse from my life, my family, and my physical and spiritual seed. Nail the curse to the cross of Jesus Christ, and render it null and void.

Father, I proclaim my dependence on you. I want to live by faith, to depend on you, and to possess my birthright. The spirit is willing, but the flesh is weak. I have a lifestyle of fear and a history of seeking comfort and security. Just as you did the miracle for Gideon, and as you sustained him when nobody would sustain him, sustain me when I have to pursue my birthright and nobody understands and sustains me. Save me not only from the enemy but also from myself.

At every place where the enemy used to curse and where you desire to release blessings, let your will be done. Release the blessings that you have decreed for me in the seasons that you decree. I pray for Israel with the giver gift, that you would protect them from the evil one and that you would bring them to true spiritual liberty from all curses. Have mercy on giver cities and nations and release the riches there, so that the people of God in this season can be restored to the fullness of their birthright. Thank you in advance for sanctifying time for me and for my generations. In Jesus' name, amen.

Blessing Of Job

The Midianite curse prevents you from accruing the capital needed to produce change through leverage, not labor. Breaking the curse stops the devouring of that which is accumulated through your labor. The blessing of Job is the freedom to accumulate resources from year to year and from generation to generation so there are enough assets to allow and cause major changes. The blessing of Job causes the family and the extended web of relationships to be supernaturally life-giving. It causes resources to multiply supernaturally, speeding the process of accumulation. God brought all of Job's relatives and his friends to him after the devouring was over. They each gave him a piece of silver and a gold ring. In terms of investment capital, that wasn't much to start with, but under the blessing of God, he leveraged that into greater wealth than he had before everything was taken from him. Job embraced the pain, and God gave him the capital to do what he needed to do. The blessing of Job is not about accrual of capital but the restoration of what was lost. God reimbursed Job everywhere there was loss. Psalm 23:1 says, "The Lord is my shepherd ... he restores my soul." God wants to restore everywhere the enemy has devoured.

Signs Of The Blessing Of Job

- Restoration and blessing flow in the areas that were previously devoured.

- Seasons that were known as seasons of loss are now seasons of unusual blessing.

How To Develop In The Blessing Of Job

- Celebrate the times when God used pain to ultimately bring you more joy and more into your calling. Focus on times when you voluntarily embraced pain to posses your calling.

- Acknowledge the things that God has given you. Celebrate the times when something was taken from you and God reimbursed you for what was lost.

- Are you making soft choices or compromising regarding sin in order to enjoy immediate comfort? One area where most Christians do this is in regard to media. Job made a covenant with his eyes (Job 31:1). Try doing the same thing by taking a 90-day media fast from CDs, music, TV, news, movies, radio, etc. After 90 days see how your spirit is. You will most likely see that it has improved tremendously.

- Job endured tremendous amounts of pain, trusting that God was in control. How long can you endure pain? How long can you let God be God while keeping your focus on what he is calling you to do? How long can you embrace the pain and trust that he is doing the right thing? Read about people who embrace pain to do kingdom work. The question is what price are you willing to pay to embrace all that God has for you?

Sevens In Scripture

Creation

The fifth day of creation parallels the gift of giver. On the fifth day God created the birds and fish. It is a day of great diversity. God has designed the giver to have widespread interests and to be involved in many things. On the negative side, givers have a propensity to get so involved in so many things, they do not bring closure to anything. God delights in the giver's diverse interests, but their strength becomes a weakness when they abandon things without getting closure, without bringing them to birth.

On this day life in the blood came into the world. The giver has a concern about health and life. They are concerned about the preservation of life, the quality of life, and being prepared for old age. Givers have a need for safety. They have an immense birthing anointing and capacity to nurture new things. The sun, moon, and stars do not birth or nurture. Trees reproduce, but it is haphazard. Trees don't nurture; they just cast their seed to the wind. So there was no nurture in the world until the fifth day. Birds and fish give birth to offspring that give birth to offspring. Birds and fish nurture their young, preparing them to carry on in the next generation. It is easy for the giver to begin something new. Givers have a strong nurturing drive and desire to care for their family. There is a generational anointing. There is birthing that leads to birthing that leads to birthing. They also desire to gather the family together for celebrations.

The fifth day of creation is also the first time God spoke blessing. Givers are called by God to reinstate the lost art of blessing. Givers desire to leave a legacy. God said to Abraham "… in you all the families of the earth shall be blessed" (Genesis 12:1-3). God designed the giver to release generational blessings into their family line and to be life-givers to others through the power of blessing.

Items Of Furniture In The Tabernacle

The fifth item of furniture is the altar of incense (Exodus 30:1-10, 37:25-28). The altar brings together intercession and worship in a single act. Worship and intercession are central in the DNA of the giver, but they must flow from relationship, not religious observance. God does not want the giver's busyness or sacrifice. God wants their heart. Gratitude tends to be hard for the giver. A proper attitude of worship is birthed out of relationship. The mature giver will worship with gratitude that comes from their relationship with God. God continually commanded the nation of Israel to remember, to celebrate the past, to look where his hand intervened for them. The giver's worship and intercession must be rooted in intentionally looking for and seeing God's fingerprints on every part of life.

Compound Names Of Jehovah

The fifth compound name of Jehovah is Jehovah-Rohi, "The Lord is my shepherd" in Psalm 23. The word *shepherd* means to tend the flock, to rule, to associate with, to feed, or to pastor. Psalm 23 pictures how God provides givers with an environment of provision, security, safety, and nurture in which to enjoy his provision. God also allows problems to intrude in the "valley of the shadow of death," so that givers can overcome fear and find comfort and security

101

In God's presence, instead of his own resources and strength. One of the giver's greatest strengths, independence, can also be his greatest weakness, if he does not find his comfort and security in God. This can keep a giver from possessing his birthright. Psalm 23:5-6 pictures God bestowing an extravagant anointing on the giver. God designed blessing to flow through a friendship relationship between the giver and God.

Seven Last Sayings On The Cross

Each one of the seven sayings parallels a challenge for that redemptive gift. The fifth saying of Christ on the cross was "I thirst." It is difficult for the giver to express need and to receive. God makes the giver to be independent, to be unmoved by pressures around them. That is good, but if it is not kept in balance, it can produce an unholy independence from God and others. At times the giver does without, rather than express a need and receive the perceived humiliation of asking and being denied. God brings the giver to the point of need to teach him how to receive greater treasures from his hand. God desires to give the giver godly resources to do his work. Sometimes God has to break givers down to personal neediness before they will receive from his hand. Givers want to give, to be life-givers, to empower others, to provide the resources that others need to possess their birthright. Givers must use that strength to combat their greatest weakness, a desire to be independent, to not be needy, to not depend on anybody.

Seven Letters To The Churches In Revelation

The gift of giver parallels the church of Sardis in Revelation 3:1-6.
I know your deeds; you have a reputation of being alive, but you are dead. Giver are rarely overtly evil. They do religious and right things, but not always with a heart for pursuing God. *Wake up! Strengthen what remains and is about to die, for I have not found your deeds complete in the sight of God.* Givers point to what they do; God points to what is lacking, what they haven't done. *Yet you have a few people in Sardis who have not soiled their clothes. They will walk with me, dressed in white, for they are worthy.* In Revelation 3 God commends those who focused on holiness. God designed givers to be concerned about appearances and reputation. The downside is that givers can craft a reputation without substance. Righteous givers are careful of their reputation. Givers serves as a guardian of reputation and are careful not to gossip. Givers understand the importance of presentation and highlight what is good and righteous and commendable in other people. God desires to wash every spot, stain, wrinkle, and blemish off his bride. *I will never blot out his name from the Book of Life, but will acknowledge his name before my Father and his angels*. Givers tend not to feel as deeply included, involved, and welcomed as they would like to be. They have many friends, acquaintances, and family, but there seems to be an insatiable longing for more and deeper relationship. Givers know that there is some kind of connectedness that is beyond what they are experiencing. That is the connectedness of their spirit and the heavenly realm. Givers have a generational worldview. They desire to leave a legacy. The Lord promises to never blot out the name of the giver who lives righteously.

Blessing Prayer For Giver

Giver, God chose you in Christ before the creation of the world to be who you are and to be gifted just as you are. You are not as out front as some of the other gifts, but they need you. I bless you to be enriched and enlarged in God's design of you and to come into alignment with his plans for you. God loves your gift, and he celebrates the complexity of your life. I bless you for your diversity. You have done many things, and yet you would like to do, know how to do, and can do many more things. You are involved in many projects, interests, and activities. You are adaptable and flexible. You do not fit easily into stereotypes or molds.

I bless your nurturing and celebrating family, your desire to have family comfortable in relationship. Nurture is a big component of your gift. It is an expression of the nature of God. I bless you as you release into your family line everything that God has in the gold mine of your inheritance. You have the God-given calling to weave people together into a relational culture, into a dynamic that is greater than the sum of its parts. I bless you with representing the heart of the Father who is a God of community. You represent his desire to create, nurture, and sustain community because you are made in his image. God delights in your desire to be life-giving to the family, to the community of faith, and to the world around you.

I bless your desire, ability, and authority to birth, nurture, and protect new ideas and new things. The prophet gift needs you for the synergy released when you and the prophet team together in the alignment and timing that God has designed for the two of you. Receive the way that God made you to contribute to his life in the body of Christ.

I bless your generational worldview. You are focused on preparing the way for others after you. God designed you to release generational blessings. God calls you to bless and to raise blessing to a high level. You fulfill your birthright when you invoke life-giving generational blessings for your family and community and produce life-giving systems that express God's design.

I bless your alertness and creativity to see options, opportunities, and possibilities that others miss. You are opportunistic in seizing the moment. I bless your success in less than ideal circumstances where all the resources are not available. I bless you to maximize imperfect environments or skill sets and create something new and lasting, finding the win-win proposition for yourself and others at the same time.

I bless your hearts desire to see people saved and the kingdom of God expanded as a eternal generational inheritance. The synergy of the kingdom is complete as you help other gifts bring unbelievers into the kingdom by providing the resources and identifying fruit that is ripe for picking.

I bless you for your independence and how you stand alone. It is a positive trait when it partners with acknowledging your need of God. Independence can be very powerful when it is

103

totally surrendered to God and in partnership with him. Pride in personal competence is a challenging occupational hazard of the giver gift. I bless you with the ability to overcome the temptation of considering yourself to be self-contained, having the authority, the money, the influence, the resources, and/or the security to do whatever you feel led to do. I bless you to be vigilant and not to let this strength be corrupted into control, which is a perversion of your gift.

I bless your strong desire to maintain your own uniqueness, but I bless you with understanding the interdependence of the gifts personally and in the community of faith. Focus on what you have to add to the other gifts with the cooperation, partnership, alignment, and synergy that God intends. Trust God to work in them to accomplish a win-win proposition with all the gifts.

I bless you with understanding and an awareness of where your gift gets tripped up. I bless you with healing of the wounds that have caused your basic trust to be fractured and caused you to respond out of woundedness. I bless you to grow into your greatest potential living in the authority and honor of the giver gift.

I bless you to win the battle of gratitude. God commanded the giver nation of Israel to remember and to celebrate his presence, his works, and his wonders. I bless you with the desire to celebrate God's past intervention. I bless you with the foundation of worship, a lifestyle of looking for and seeing God's fingerprints on every part of life. I bless your leading others to recognize the work of God and calling attention to him as he provides big things and little things.

I bless you as a networker, bringing people together, persuading and inspiring people to do things that they would not normally do. Nobody networks like the giver, and you delight in introducing people and building through relationship. Develop your gift of being intentionally life-giving from your spirit to the spirit of others.

Giver, you are pragmatic and a practical peacemaker. You are not confrontational by nature. You are diplomatic, not wanting to offend. In dealing with people, you get disproportionate return on your effort. You can work with people who have conflicting views and theologies for the sake of a group or a project. You relate to a wide range of very different people. It is as if you are the hub of a wheel, and the spokes radiate out from you. Without the hub, the wheel could not move forward to accomplish a God-given objective. I bless your ability in the community of believers to keep the other gifts related and properly focused.

You are careful of your reputation and that of others. You speak of what is good, righteous, and commendable in other people. I bless your caring about the reputation of the kingdom and of the bride of Christ.

You resist manipulation of information. You don't like to have anything withheld from you. You have an intuitive sense for what is false. I bless your gift of discernment in this area.

You usually do the right things, and your acquaintances would say of you that you are a nice person. I bless you to go deeper with God and deepen your spiritual motivation of holiness, which is pleasing to him.

104

You find favor in money and resources flowing to you without human explanation or reason. You find bargains, and people give you discounts. At times you may find yourself fighting the temptation to use money as a point of security or as a means of gratification, entitlement, reward, or control. I bless your spirit with the ability to overcome these temptations.

I bless you to give well and wisely where there is the greatest potential for eternal return on your investment. When your giving is exercised with God's wisdom, it makes others grateful for God's generosity, and he gets the credit and the glory. I bless you with learning how to give in ways that nurture the spirit to form a deeper and richer community.

You tend not to see patterns from the past. You also tend to rationalize and often to blame. You resent it when someone confronts you over issues that are more than a week old. I bless you with the ability to learn from life experiences and see things from God's perspective. I bless you with the ability to react with grace when others point out patterns that you do not see.

I bless you with being secure because of your relationship with God. I bless you with letting God take your faith to new levels. Sometimes faith is hard for you, because you want to avoid risk, and it may lead to fear and control. I bless you with winning the battle against control. It's not God's design for you to play it safe and only do the things that you are sure that you can handle. I bless you with faith that is greater than fear of risk.

Stewardship is the essence of living by faith. You receive resources from God to do what he calls you to do. God's standard for the giver is stewardship of all, because everything belongs to him. The principle of stewardship relates to life, potential, gifts, resources, and relationships. It extends to long-term life-giving generational changes. You are meant to establish relationship and invest in generational blessings that you will pass on. I bless you with being the model of a steward of everything God gives.

I bless you with being settled in who you are in Christ, your identity in him, and your legitimacy as a covenant child of the King of kings, as you partner with him in intimate relationship.

You are meant to interface powerfully with the other gifts. The community of the gifts needs you to possess your birthright in your unique way. That is the dignity, honor, and beauty of the God-seeking giver. You are God's choice for some significant things. I bless you with moving into your full birthright.

Ruler

The ruler is God's empire-builder. The ruler is an administrator, a leader, and an implementer. He is willing to own his own problems and fix them. Under God's direction, he can significantly expand the work of God. Rulers thrive under pressure, can motivate others, and are independent. Rulers need to learn that although they don't need others, others need them to invest in fathering and nurturing those in their care (or on their team), so others can develop as God intended for them. Rulers can use imperfect people and tolerate a level of compromise. Failure to seek God's direction will cause rulers to accomplish many good things, but not God's best, and end their life with a sense of futility like Solomon. While rulers can be very busy, the question is are they doing what God called them to do? They are commonly seen as people who establish organizations and put people in order. However, the true birthright of rulers is to establish generational blessings for their family and ministry that outlast their life.

Biblical Examples Of Ruler: Boaz, Joseph, Nehemiah, and Solomon.

Principle Of Freedom

The principle of freedom parallels the gift of ruler. Freedom is the fruit of effectively weaving together resources, principles, and blessings to move toward your birthright. The principle of freedom is knowing how to fight and how to build. In fighting you have to learn how to weave together resources, principles, and blessings to move out of bondage into the positive numbers. Once you are in the positive numbers, you need to know how to weave together resources, principles, and blessings to build into your society. Everyone needs to leave a deposit behind them that is greater than the resources that they've used up during their lifetime. Everybody needs to leave a larger deposit for their children than what they inherited from their fathers. Each person needs to leave the world a better place.

True freedom is achieved as four elements come together. Those elements are (1) submitting to God's agenda, (2) looking at the resources and identifying the raw materials God has given, (3) studying the principles to learn how to assemble them, and (4) expecting God's intervention in the form of blessings. Each of these activities is a different facet of building. All of these elements require three factors: resources, principles, and/or blessings. Most people default to one of the three. Freedom comes from seeing a vast array of resources and knowing when and how to use them. Freedom comes from having your toolbox full of biblical principles that can be applied selectively, weaving together multiple principles at any given time. Freedom comes when you can access a wide range of God's blessings to build his kingdom.

Authority Of Ruler

- To live in the highest level of generational anointing.

- To reclaim dominion of the earth.

- To impart blessings to bring freedom.

Birthright Of Ruler

- Release spiritual generational blessings to their physical and spiritual seed.

- Go beyond obedience and honor God.

- Seek God for his desire.

- Live in freedom and holiness.

Number Line For Scale Of Responsibility For Ruler

+100 **Complete restoration.** Extending Eden on a global scale. Isaiah 11:6-10; 41:17-20

+80 **Restoring devastation.** Looking for wreckage and seeking to restore it in an individual or institution. For example, Nehemiah in the restoration of Jerusalem.

+60 **Applying the principle of freedom to an institution.** Pursuing personal birthright and blessing the community around you (churches, businesses, schools, etc.).

+40 **Applying God's principles to the family.** Ability to live for personal calling and for the next generation at the same time. Multi-generational focus. Meshing personal calling with the calling of the children.

+20 **Committed to the process of God's agenda.** Has identified the resources God has placed in and around them. Knowing God's principles and how to operate in them and expecting God to grant his blessing personally.

0 **Ordinary Christian.** No overt bondage. Generally godly and has personal, moral, and financial freedom. Gives a little more than they take.

-20 **Poverty spirit.** Unable to see resources around or within themselves. Focused on the next fix or instant relief, not on moving forward.

-40 **Personal bondage.** People living in chronic bondage, addiction, "bad luck," etc. Their issues spill over and effect those around them. For example, alcoholic parent who causes children to feel the consequences of bondage to addiction.

-60 **Institutional predatory leadership.** Leaders who exploit their followers in businesses, schools, church, sports enterprises, etc.

-80 **National exploitation that results in national bondage.** Demonic control brought by curses or violation of God's principles. Leader is not overtly dedicating his nation to evil, but by his leadership he produces curses that have the same effect.

-100 **Demonic control by a covenant.** Intentional public dedication of a nation to the demonic. Intentionally God's will and relying instead on Satanic resources on a national scale. Or an influential person in a government practices Freemasonry or some other form of Luciferianism.

109

Jotham's Curse

Biblical Basis: Judges 9

Jerub-Baal was the rightful leader of Shechem. Jerub-Baal had 70 sons. His nephew Abimelch went behind his back to the people and convinced them that it would be better to kill all 70 sons and make Abimelch the leader. He convinced the people to revolt with him, and they killed the sons, except for the youngest son, Jotham, who escaped. Abimelch became king, but Jotham returned and said to the citizens, *Now if you have acted honorably and in good faith when you made Abimelech king, and if you have been fair to Jerub-Baal and his family, and if you have treated him as he deserves and to think that my father fought for you, risked his life to rescue you from the hand of Midian… if then you have acted honorably and in good faith toward Jerub-Baal and his family today, may Abimelech be your joy, and may you be his, too! But if you have not, let fire come out from Abimelech and consume you, citizens of Shechem and Beth Millo, and let fire come out from you, citizens of Shechem and Beth Millo, and consume Abimelech!*

When Abimelech heard that the citizens were assembling, he set the tower they were in on fire and killed about a thousand people. At the next tower a woman dropped a millstone on his head and killed him. Thus, God repaid the wickedness that Abimelech had done to his father by murdering his seventy brothers. God repaid the wickedness of the men of Shechem. The curse of Jotham came on them (Judges 9:55-57). Jotham told God that the people deserved to be wiped out, and if he was right, God should allow the people to destroy each other. Jotham desired to destroy their social capital (morale, organization, team dynamics, shared history, group identity). Jotham's curse causes betrayal from within an organization, usually by trusted leaders. Its goal is to destroy the momentum and group capital that has been gained.

Legitimacy Lie

"I am legitimate when I am over people, and I have institutional authority."

Signs Of The Curse

- Team or institution is destroyed by betrayal from within. The devouring is seen when the people who are supposed to be in a covenant relationship with you turn around and rob you.
- In a family there is a history of division. In every generation there are siblings or relatives who won't talk to each other. A continual pattern of division.
- In churches, a trusted leader (associate pastor, deacon, elder) who has been a trusted member of the team decides to leave the church and take members of the church with him. In ministry teams, dishonoring words are spoken about other team members.

Possible Cause

- You or somebody in your family line or institutional line violated a covenant relationship.
- You or somebody in your family line were ungrateful toward those who were good to you. You chose to discredit others to whom you owed a debt of gratitude.

Prayer Of Renunciation Of Jotham's Curse

Almighty God and heavenly Father, you are the God of covenant, of community, of institutions, and of government. You have designed human institutions to be life-giving, to be generational, and to be strategic. Institutions that deliver death instead of life are the work of the enemy and not the work of your hands. Open the books in my generational lines and show me the roots of this curse. I confess, reject, and renounce the sins of ingratitude to those who have been life-givers to me. I confess the sin of covenant-breaking regarding life-giving relationships. I confess, reject, and renounce the sins of sedition and lawlessness. I repudiate the lie that legitimacy can come from having power through an institution.

Father, you have designed some institutions to have great power. You use institutions to transform societies, but I reject the deception that legitimacy comes through institutional power. I have seen the curse of Jotham operating in my life and in my culture. The death that it brings is painful, and yet you are a just God, and you only empower Jotham's curse where there has been covenant-breaking. So I accept the justice of your judgment.

Father, I embrace the justice of your restoration. Because of the blood of the Lamb and the word of my confession, those iniquities are now under the blood, and the enemy is disempowered. In the name of Jesus Christ of Nazareth, I command every demonic entity that has been operating through Jotham's curse to leave me, my family line, my ministry, my business, and my physical and spiritual seed to a thousand generations. Teach me about covenant, and empower me to be a covenant-keeper. Release the blessing of freedom of movement in my life so that I walk on a smooth road.

I bless the institutions that you have chosen for me. Give me your grace to stay in covenant with those who are covenant-breakers. Give me the grace to finish the course that you have laid out for me. Release the blessings that have been blocked that are rightfully mine. Release them into my life, my family, my ministry, my business, and my institutions. I ask this in the name of Jesus Christ, because he kept covenant and finished his course. Amen.

Blessing Of Nehemiah

Jotham's curse causes betrayal from within an organization, usually by trusted leaders. When the curse is broken, there can be a stable organization that grows normally. When Nehemiah's blessing is operating, the social structures are supernaturally, synergistically life giving. Nehemiah demonstrated this by building the wall of Jerusalem with people who were not builders, who had no previous relationship with him, and who had every reason to fail at their task. Because the blessing was flowing through him, ordinary people worked as a team doing something they had never done before, and they got a hugely disproportionate result for their effort. Their minimal skills meshed in a supernatural way to produce an outstanding result. When substantial capital is married to a synergistically life-giving social structure, the impact in the world is massive.

Signs Of The Blessing Of Nehemiah

- Ability to establish a social structure that synergistically releases life into your calling and culture. You might be able to possess your birthright alone, but you cannot be a person of destiny outside of community.

How To Develop In The Blessing Of Nehemiah

- Think of those who have been life-giving to you in a major way. Have you destroyed, dishonored, reviled, or exposed those who have been life-giving to you? Make a list of those whom God used to build things into you that you continue to use for years, especially those who later hurt you or defrauded you. Thank God for the ways they built into you, although they hurt you. We can focus on the fact that we have been defrauded and miss the goodness of God.

- Celebrate the times that God sent people to build you up.

- Embrace a lifestyle of honoring the spiritual awakening and growth process in others, as well as their godly character and wisdom (not skill).

Sevens In Scripture

Creation

The sixth day of creation parallels the gift of ruler. On the sixth day God made animals, insects, and human beings. God told Adam and Eve to take dominion over the earth. He blessed them and said to them, "Be fruitful and increase in number; fill the earth and subdue it. Rule over the fish of the sea and the birds of the air and over every living creature that moves on the ground" (Genesis 1:28). Dominion over other people may be assumed, perhaps, but God did not say that on the sixth day. God designed rulers to organize and administer social units, groups of people and resources and to live in dominion over creation. Psalm 8:6-8 says, "You made him (man) ruler over the works of your hands; you put everything under his feet: all flocks and herds, and the beasts of the field, the birds of the air, and the fish of the sea, all that swim the paths of the seas." Rulers have a wonderful ability to mobilize many people to accomplish a task. They understand when to push people, when to inspire them, when to command them, and when to lead. Also on this day God breathed the breath of life into the first man, creating the human spirit. As good as rulers are at dealing with logistics, structure, people, and projects, the ruler's call is to the human spirit. Rulers are made in the image of God and are made to father people's spirits. The ruler's call is to nurture the human spirit, to weave together a community based on oneness of spirit, and to lead the spirit with God-given dominion toward the goals of God.

Items Of Furniture In The Tabernacle

The sixth item of furniture is the ark of the covenant (Exodus 25:10-16; 37:1-5). Inside the ark, there were three things that represent the basis of a ruler's authority of leading a human community.

1. The law. The ruler needs to be submitted to the law of God, because all human authority is derived from submission. One must be submitted to God before he has legal right to exercise authority over others.

2. A golden pot of manna. Manna was God's life-sustaining provision for Israel. A ruler has a moral right to lead when he can provide for those who follow, when life flows from him to them.

3. Aaron's rod that budded. The first two items preceded Aaron's rod by a significant period of time. God spoke and appointed the Levitical tribe to their task because of carnality and rebellion in the camp. It represents the sovereign appointment to an office by God.

True leadership is not based on our title or our position in a structure. It is based on the degree to which someone is submitted to God's law and is life-giving to those around them. Rulers must choose to receive their authority from submission to God's Word, rather than relying on human power and manipulation. This is an area where rulers tend to compromise, believing that the ends justify the means. As rulers submit to God's authority, their moral and spiritual authority will grow. Rather than using human power to achieve greatness, rulers must allow God to be the one to say, "This is my appointed leader."

113

Compound Names Of Jehovah

The sixth of the compound names of Jehovah is Jehovah-Tsidkenu, "The Lord our Righteousness" (Jeremiah 23:5-6). Righteousness is an unswerving adherence to God's standard of what is right. Righteousness is the battlefield of rulers. Rulers must choose to rule by righteousness instead of manipulation, bribery, or compromise. Truly effective rulers possess character enough to take a stand on righteousness even if it costs them. The individual righteousness of rulers is the foundation from which their dominion and authority flow.

Seven Last Sayings On The Cross

Each one of the seven sayings of Christ on the cross parallels a challenge for that redemptive gift. The sixth thing that Christ said on the cross was, "It is finished." He was referring to paying the price for sin. When we come to the Father for salvation, we receive justice, not just mercy or grace. We receive justice because Jesus Christ has paid in full for every one of our sins. God is not merely choosing to look the other way or bend the rules, the payment has been made. As rulers apply this truth to their own lives, realizing that there is nothing they have "to do" to stand righteously before God, they will come into a large place of freedom.

It is easy for rulers to absorb themselves and invest their lives in the visible and the tangible. The issue is not whether rulers are productive or busy, but whether they are doing the thing that God called them to do. Solomon is an example of someone who was very busy with many good and tangible things. He had wealth, fame, reputation, resources, priests, worshipers, and a large army, and he established peace in the land. Yet, he had the potential to make a major impact for the kingdom beyond his many achievements. Everyone around the world heard about the king of Israel through commerce. But God's call was for people to hear about the God of the king of Israel, not just about Solomon's achievements. In this sense, Solomon missed out on an important part of his birthright.

Looking at Christ, by contrast, it would have been easy for him to amass a following, to organize a group of leaders, and to establish an army to drive out the Romans. He could have cleansed the temple and changed the priesthood. Instead, he poured his life into the spiritual dimension, not the natural one. He deliberately left the crowds. He withdrew from Israel several times. He went to the cross instead of taking the momentum of Palm Sunday and overthrowing everything that was evil and wicked. Because Jesus invested his best effort into the one thing he was called to do, he paid for all sins past, present, and future, and we can have freedom.

The greatest gift that rulers give is freedom, but it comes at a price. That price is backing off from the social structures that they can build in order to focus on the spiritual structures. Rulers must step into the greatness that God has called them to, avoiding the seduction of the soul and culture, becoming passionate about cleansing their spiritual line and building a spiritual heritage for their physical and spiritual seed. This is the lasting heritage that Jesus Christ left for all rulers.

Seven Letters To The Churches In Revelation

The redemptive gift of ruler parallels the church of Philadelphia in Revelation 3:7-13 NKJV. **"These things says He who is holy, He who is true…"** Righteousness and holiness are the issues on which rulers will rise or fall.

"I know your works. See, I have set before you an open door and no one can shut it; for you have a little strength, have kept My word, and have not denied My name." God blesses the righteous ruler. When rulers are going through the door that God has opened for them, there is a grace upon them to find resources that other people don't see, and they weave together resources to make an impact that is disproportionate to the resources they have at their disposal.

"Indeed I will make those of the synagogue of Satan, who say they are Jews and are not, but lie— indeed I will make them come and worship before your feet, and to know that I have loved you." Rulers know and rest on the Word of God. Rulers do not need the validation or affirmation of others. When they have made up their mind that they are called to do something, they can do it even if no one is affirming them. The only validation a ruler needs is validation from God.

"Because you kept my command to endure patiently, I will also keep you from the hour of trial." When other churches were destroyed during the Islamic invasion, God preserved this church with supernatural protection. God's desire for rulers is to go beyond the natural to partnering with him and accomplishing that which only he can do, leaving a generational impact.

Blessing Prayer For Ruler

I bless your leadership call to organize and administer social units, groups of people, and resources. Your maximum leadership quotient is based on God's gifting, being submitted to God's law, and being life-giving to those around you. I bless you as an implementer who takes a vision and effectively implements a plan from incremental steps. You know the resources available and needed to reach a goal. You can visualize the final result of a major undertaking by a group, and at the same time break down major goals into smaller achievable tasks for individuals, as Nehemiah did. I bless how you pull together a group based on loyalty to own a problem together. You need loyalty and confidence from those who are being directed and served.

I bless your strength of seeing the opportunity to use imperfect, broken people and position them to draw the best out of them without letting their brokenness damage the whole. I bless how you position others for success while minimizing their weaknesses that would hinder a project. You can overlook character faults and woundedness, inexperience, immaturity in people who otherwise have valuable skills to offer in reaching the goal. I bless you for bringing out of people the very best that they can contribute to the whole group.

I bless your ability to know what you should and should not delegate to others. You can orchestrate the details by delegating, and you do not involve yourself in details in order to focus on the ultimate goal.

I bless your ability to thrive under pressure and also to motivate people to do more than they think they can do. I bless how you challenge people to go beyond anything they have done before, but you are sensitive to know when you are putting other people under too much pressure. Jesus has given you the life-giving treasure of himself in you with which to be life-giving, even when you are expecting people to go beyond where they have ever been.

God has given you the gift of being task-oriented, focused on the objective. I bless your ability to endure reaction from insiders and outsiders to reach a higher envisioned goal, as you appropriately balance suggestions, appeals, and valid complaints of those on the team. I bless you to be totally in tune with God and doing what he says to do. You do not need the affirmation of other people when you've heard from God. You can receive your vindication from God and wait a long time for it. Your example is Jesus, who was willing to be humbled and accepted the reviling of others to bring freedom to the world. He endured the scorn, despising the shame (Hebrews 12:2), when sinful men tortured him and crucified him, thus bringing salvation to us.

Some will not appreciate the work that you are doing or the way you are doing it. Some will resist and resent you, and others will be jealous of you. I bless you to carry on, because God has designed you to be less influenced by public opinion than most. You can endure opposition and criticism by those over, under, and around you. I bless you to press on when people who should support you don't.

I bless you as you inspire and encourage a team through cheerfulness, approval, praise, challenge, personal sensitivity, and nurture. I bless you to give explanation to each strategic part of individual roles in the big picture. Everybody needs to know that their role is vital, even indispensable, and where their contribution fits into the overall scheme. I bless you to not overlook individual needs of workers and not to view them as resources, as pieces on a chessboard to accomplish goals or tasks. I bless you to shepherd people. It is a beautiful part of being a ruler when you see your call to shepherd the people who are involved in the organization or objective at hand.

I bless your independence in a positive way. You have no welfare mentality. You don't look to others for solutions. You are not into blame, either yourself or others. I bless your strength of figuring out how to fix it when something goes wrong. You are willing to own problems and accomplish the task rather than wasting time blaming and assigning fault.

I bless you with a singleness of heart and the ability to focus on what God has called you to do. The result of your godly work is disproportionate to the investment of resources. The example of Nehemiah is your heritage as a ruler. You get results that are beyond brilliant administrative skills when you are partnering with God, doing the main thing or the one thing he has called you to do.

I bless how you see the open door God places before you and use inadequate resources to accomplish extraordinary things. This is how God made you, and it brings him pleasure when you accomplish that. When you are following God, at the right place, at the right time, doing the right thing, God's grace is upon you to find resources that others don't see and weave them together for a hugely disproportionate impact. Your Father is pleased when you do the impossible, so that he gets the glory when the only explanation for it is "God was in it." He is tapping deep into what he placed within you, and your Father delights in watching you in operation. That is his great joy.

I bless you to pursue the full range of dominion that God intended for you. You are so gifted and talented in the natural, that it would take two lifetimes to do everything you are good at. You look at anything and want to make it bigger and better. Beware of the danger of success, when you are talented and gifted enough to succeed on your merits. Your success can become a trap as you camp out on success when God wants you to partner in the spiritual realm and do the supernatural, and accomplish what only God can do.

I bless your diversity. You have your finger many pies, and you do it with great skill and grace. You seem to be good at everything you touch. You organize and you lead. You see opportunities and possibilities. There are things you may do that will bring you pleasure and leave a legacy in your community. Nevertheless, the good is the eternal enemy of the best. Sometimes you can settle for man's plans and fall short of God's design. Jesus is your model, as he finished the one thing his Father sent him to do (John 17:4). On the cross Jesus said, "It is finished." He got the key thing done. There is no greater satisfaction at the end of the day or of a lifetime,

117

than to know that you have glorified your Father by doing exactly what he wanted you to do. I bless you to find your greatest fulfillment there, as his kingdom will be extended, and the world will be changed for generations to come.

A potential weakness of your gift is compromise, settling for what is OK instead of God's best. That is not God's highest and best for you. God designed you for living in righteousness, holiness, and life-giving. On these values you stand or fall. I bless you to use the moral authority that comes from submitting to God as the basis of your authority. Where you have integrity, you will have spiritual authority, greater influence, and everything necessary to lead people. As you do that, your moral and spiritual authority will grow and you will give life to your community as the righteous leader God wants you to be.

I bless your joy and fulfillment in seeing all the parts come together in a finished product. Hebrews 12 says that for the joy set before him, Jesus endured the cross where he paid in full the total legal penalty for sin. Because of that finished work on the cross, we have freedom. I bless you to live in freedom and fight for freedom for others. I bless you in the principle of freedom that is the fruit of effectively weaving together resources, principles, and blessings to move toward your birthright. I bless you in the fullness of your calling to show the world what freedom can be.

I bless your God-given authority in a high level of generational anointing. You desire to impart generational blessings. God's call is for you to concern yourself with the spirit realm in your family, purging and cleansing the generational lines and building a generational blessing and heritage for the generations after you. Your birthright is to invest in a community of faith and to cleanse others from the defilement coming down from their ancestors, to build a deposit of blessing that will carry them for generations after you leave. I bless you as you step into the greatness that God has called you to and become passionate about cleansing your spiritual line and building a spiritual heritage for your physical and spiritual seed. You were made to leave a great spiritual heritage as you accrue a high level of spiritual dominion over spiritual issues and pass on to your physical and spiritual offspring generational blessings that will pursue them all their days.

I bless you with expanding your thinking about your gift. It is more than dominion over people as of a leader of organizations. That is a portion of your birthright, but that is not the original mandate of God. Based on the sixth day of creation, God designed you for dominion over the animal kingdom, although you have not lived it yet. Your birthright is to set the spiritual dynamic of the day and to call the right living creatures to do the right thing, whether in motion, or sound, or color, etc. You may be nowhere near there yet, but I bless you with releasing what God has placed in you that has been carried for hundreds of generations since Adam and Eve without seeing its full expression. I bless you in your generation with unleashing the power that God has placed in creation. I bless you with living in the original blessing that God gave to you, son of Adam and son of the Second Adam.

As a ruler you may not have developed in your capacity for fathering and leading the human spirit. On the sixth day of creation God created the human spirit and placed it in the first man. The spirit is the righteous domain of the ruler, not just command and power and control. I bless you as you grow and become accomplished in your spiritual DNA of leading the spirits of others. I bless your capacity for fathering the human spirit, for knowing when to build and when to war, that comes with your gift. You are called to know more about how to guide, lead, shape, and use the spirit, as well as the soul. I bless your call to father by nurturing the human spirit, not just the soul. I bless you in your challenge to understand the spirit as profoundly as you understand the soul. I bless you as you nurture your spirit and rely on the power of heaven to supplement what you can do in the natural. Mobilize the spirits of people— leading, grouping, deploying their spirits. Create the synergy of one person's spirit with another, of one team's spirit with another team's spirit. You were made to father the spirit, not just the soul. I bless you as you understand how to bless the human spirit for the good of the kingdom of God. I bless you as you live in your anointing to nurture the human spirit and weave together a human community based on oneness of spirit, not common goals for the soul. When the spirit is dominant, it draws out the best of the soul. The soul operates at a better level when it is under the leadership of the spirit. I bless you to use the resources of the spirit and the resources of heaven in fathering the next generation.

Mercy

Mercy is the crown jewel of the gifts. For the mercy worship is crucial. It's in his DNA. He comes into God's presence in worship and then leads others into his presence at a very intimate level. Worship is cleansing and brings holiness to the rest of the body, making the bride of Christ pure. The mercy gift frequently expresses worship and pain artistically. Mercy is designed primarily to **be,** not to **do**. The gift of mercy feels life and does not just do life. Mercy moves at a slower speed because God designed him to extract the deepest amount of insight, understanding, and wisdom from what he sees. He has the highest authority for ministering to the wounded. He speaks the language of love. He absorbs pain and tension around him and can become burden-bearers for others. He is easily hurt and has difficulty processing and healing from injury. Mercy develops protective structures for dealing with pain. Mercy celebrates what is good, right, and true. He is alert to and aware of the parts and the whole. He is sensitive to things being out of place. He recognizes alignment when all the pieces are in their right relationship. Mercy must realize that he thinks, processes, and feels differently than others. People around him will try to change the mercy and make him fit into a more "acceptable" mold. Once the mercy is released to be who God has designed him to be, the things that he does will have a whole different flavor.

Biblical Examples Of Mercy: Adam, David, and John.

Principle Of Fulfillment

The principle that parallels the gift of mercy is fulfillment. Fulfillment is using all of your abilities to do what God designed you to do. Ephesians 2:10 says we are God's workmanship. We are his masterpiece, created in Christ Jesus to do good works which God prepared in advance for us to do. God has uniquely designed each person to do a set of good works. God gave a different set of works to Paul than he gave to Moses, David, or John. Each of them were designed for their set of works. You are God's best design for the works he has prepared for you.

Fulfillment is not the same as happiness. Our culture generally defines happiness as either not having problems or having enough money to pay somebody to take care of the problems. But happiness is not the primary goal of life. God illustrated this principle in the Garden of Eden. Adam and Eve were in paradise, but in order for them to experience fulfillment, God gave them a problem to solve. He told them to be fruitful and multiply. God knew that they had the capacity to learn a massive amount of information to solve the problems that he presented them, because he had interwoven it into their very being. Without the pressure of the problem to solve, they would probably not have been motivated to learn how to be fruitful. They would remain underachievers, and underachievers do not experience fulfillment. The only way to experience fulfillment is to embrace the right problems God presents us with that will cause growth. Everyone was made to solve problems.

The devil's goal is to orchestrate each person's life so that they don't have a chance to develop who they are. He keeps them busy doing many different things so they may end up frustrated, feeling futile, experiencing boredom, and not experiencing fulfillment. Jesus came to bring abundant life (John 10:10). God designed people to experience extraordinary fulfillment when they are doing what God created them to do. When the devil can create a generation of people who have sought God and ended up frustrated, experiencing futility in their lives, he has won great honor for himself. In order to achieve fulfillment a person must (1) discover who they are and what problems they are supposed to solve, (2) hone their problem-solving skill in that area, and (3) enjoy life while solving the problems that God designed them to solve.

Authority Of Mercy

- To sanctify time through blessing.
- To know the heart of God.
- To live in a degree of holiness in order to impart it and make holy what is defiled.
- To experience intimacy with God in an easier and deeper way so that it can be released.

Birthright of Mercy

- To live in dominion over sin and unholy circumstances.
- To release the holiness and glory of God into their environment.
- To "BE" in the presence of God at all times.
- Worship (celebrate) God in all aspects of life.

Number Line For Scale Of Responsibility For Mercy, Part I

The way a mercy receives and processes information is unique and different from the other six gifts. The mercy enjoys a more circular, free-flowing expression, rather than the logic-driven, left-brained number line. This is an attempt to speak in the language of the mercy.

Following Your Passion

Nuturing Your Spirit

Discovery

Growing through problems

Fulfillment vs. Futility

Alignment

Tapping into blessings

Taking Risk

Finding Your Niche

Exploring Pleasure

123

Number Line For Scale Of Responsibility For Mercy

For the rest of the gifts, who long to understand more about the gift of mercy, here is a more traditional number line.

+100 **Fulfillment.** Engaging 100% of their abilities (spirit, soul, body) to overcome the problems and obstacles God designed for him to solve. For example, even in a perfect environment, Adam and Eve would not know fulfillment unless they solved the problem of subduing the earth. Ultimate fulfillment comes in leaving a legacy.

+80 **Bringing the community into alignment with God.** Helps the community realize its potential so it can be life-giving to its inhabitants.

+60 **Helping others discover their value and niche anointing.** Shows others how to discover what God has placed inside of them and their place in the kingdom of God.

+40 **Finding their niche.** God's desire is for mercy to know who he is, what he is to do, and what problems he is to solve (Ephesians 2:10). God's strategy is to bring him problems he doesn't know how to solve in order to force him to develop the abilities that God knows are within him. This is how he learns something about himself that he didn't know.

+20 **Exploring what brings pleasure.** Enjoys life being who God designed him to be. Begins to take risks. Begins to receive and recognize gifts from God and deal with issues of character and woundedness.

0 **Pleasing God, not man.** "Offer your bodies as living sacrifices, holy and pleasing to God—this is your spiritual act of worship. Do not conform any longer to the pattern of this world, but be transformed by the renewing of your mind. Then you will be able to test and approve what God's will is—his good, pleasing and perfect will" (Romans 12:1-2).

-20 **Man-pleasing, self-gratification, pursuing personal happiness.** Seeking identity from others and the culture rather than God.

-40 **Stubbornness.** Can be rooted in unforgiveness.

-60 **Sins of omission.** They neither glorified him as God nor give thanks to him (Romans 1:21-32). Darkened hearts and foolish thinking.

-80 **Blaming God.** Results in physical or spiritual barrenness.

-100 **Futility.** Dying without leaving a personal legacy for himself or his community.

Ammonite Curse

Biblical Basis: Judges 11

Jephthah the Gileadite was a mighty warrior. His father was Gilead; his mother was a prostitute. Gilead's wife gave him many sons. The sons drove Jephthah away so he would not get any of the inheritance, telling him he was the son of another woman. So Jephthah fled from his brothers and settled in the land of Tob. Some time later, when the Ammonites made war on Israel, the elders of Gilead went to get Jephthah and asked him to become their commander against the Ammonites. Jephthah said to them, "Didn't you hate me and drive me from my father's house? Why do you come to me now, when you're in trouble?" The elders of Gilead said to him, "Nevertheless, we are turning to you now; come with us to fight the Ammonites, and you will be our head over all who live in Gilead." Jephthah answered, "Suppose you take me back to fight the Ammonites and the Lord gives them to me—will I really be your head?" The elders of Gilead replied, "The Lord is our witness; we will certainly do as you say." The Spirit of the Lord came upon Jephthah as he advanced against the Ammonites. Jephthah made a vow to the Lord: "If you give the Ammonites into my hands, whatever comes out of the door of my house to meet me when I return in triumph from the Ammonites will be the Lord's, and I will sacrifice it as a burnt offering." Jephthah went over to fight the Ammonites, and God gave them into his hands. When Jephthah returned to his home, his daughter came out to meet him. She was his only child. When Jephthah saw her, he was distraught because of the vow he had made.

The Ammonite curse causes a person to refuse to receive the gifts of God. Physical or spiritual barrenness results. God gave Jephthah everything he needed for victory. However, he did not recognize God's gifts and demanded civil authority that God did not intend him to have. His civil leadership was deadly because he sought something God did not intend for him to prosper in. God designed Jephthah to be a mighty warrior, not a political leader. He tried to bribe God with an unnecessary sacrifice. Jephthah did not need to give God a sacrifice to have victory. In the end the results were disastrous. His only child died at his own hands, so he had no generational impact. Jephthah could not conceive of God's repayment for how he had been wronged, so he took it for himself. God had allowed him to be born of a prostitute and to live wounded to prepare him for incredible victory, but because he could not recognize the hand of God in the process, his bitterness caused him to not receive what God had for him.

Legitimacy Lie

"I am legitimate when I have earned God's or people's favor through self-sacrifice."

Signs Of The Curse

- Physical or spiritual barrenness in life, and you are unable to reproduce.
- Being confined to mediocrity.
- Losing the capital to make money. You are relegated to earning money, instead of making money. In the home, values of the parents are not reproduced.
- Practicing extreme generosity or sacrifice that is inappropriate, in order to buy people's love or God's favor.

125

Possible Cause

- You or your ancestors tried to buy God's favor. Instead of receiving God's gifts, you insisted on giving God gifts that he did not request.

- Believing that the only way to please God is with sacrifice.

- Generosity flowing from fear instead of love.

Principle Of Compensation

The key to overcoming the Ammonite curse is the principle of compensation. Everyone has pain in their lives. Some of the pain is brought on by bad choices and by sinful nature. However, at the moment of conception we had done nothing wrong. Everyone was willed into existence by God, and he chose to place them in a particular family. Some were placed into a family that was very wounding. Some were placed into families that did not nurture emotionally, physically, or spiritually. No one chose their family. The truth is that some got a bad deal from God. Jephthah was one of these people. He was the son of a prostitute and the most important man in town, and everyone knew it. Jephthah had a lousy childhood. His brothers did not like him; they disinherited him after his father died. He was forced to live in the wilderness. Where is the justice, the holiness, and the love of God when he deliberately places a person in a wounding situation through no fault of their own, and they cannot change it? The answer is found in the principle of compensation. True, Jephthah received some bad things from God which he did not deserve, but he also received some good things from God which he did not earn. God made him a mighty warrior and caused the rest of the circumstances to occur so his gifting could flourish. God created a vacuum of leadership in the nation so they had to get Jephthah to lead.

In the short term, it may appear that God has given you a bad deal, but God is always just, fair, and loving. He always supplies a repayment that is infinitely greater than the brokenness. But a lot of people are born, live, and die in brokenness. The key is in Judges 11:4, "Some time later..." God's repayment occurs at his chosen time. For Jephthah, the "some time later" was long enough to have a daughter of marrying age. God gave him that time to grow, to mature, to repair himself spiritually, but Jephthah spent his "some time later" in bitterness, self-pity, waiting to get his revenge, dreaming of the day when the judges of Gilead would need a favor and he could rub it in. Because Jephthah could not see and embrace the compensation of God and believe that there was compensation coming, he did a stupid thing. Because of his woundedness, he tried to bribe God to give him what he had already planned to give him. There was no need to bribe God. He is not unjust in the fullness of time, although he may appear unjust for a moment in time. We must learn to live through injustice without being bitter while living in expectation of God's compensation in the "some time later." For some, the repayment will not come to them but to a generation that follows them.

Prayer Of Renunciation Of The Ammonite Curse

Almighty God and heavenly Father, I rejoice in calling you Father. I come to you acknowledging that you are the Righteous Judge of the universe and my loving Father. I have been deceived, and I have acted wrongly out of my deception. I reject the lie that I need to or that I could earn your favor or your love. I reject and renounce my focus on human favor. I reject and renounce every incident in my family line where somebody chose to embrace human perspectives instead of your perspective. I reject every human stigma that is contrary to your view of me. I reject and renounce the cultural pressure that causes me to not excel, lest I make others look bad. I reject and renounce the cowardice of failing to speak up about things that are evil, lest I offend those around me. I reject and renounce the iniquity of valuing the favor of men more than possessing my birthright. Forgive me for those iniquities.

Cover those things with the blood of Jesus in every branch of my family line. Bring that cleansing from the beginning of time to the present, to my physical and spiritual seed to a thousand generations. I command every devouring spirit that has been empowered by these curses to leave now in the name of Jesus and to go and never return to me or my spiritual seed or my physical descendants.

The issue for me is to learn to love you, not for me to purchase your love. Anoint my eyes with the ointment of Revelation 3:18, so I can see your love in the daily events of my life. In every act of service to you, reveal more of your love for me. As I see your love, cause my love for you to well up within me. Create a fire within me to possess my birthright. I see in part, and I know in part. There is so much you want to show me that I am not able to receive.

Father, enlarge my spirit and my capacity to receive the passion of heaven and fill that space with the passion that Jesus had. Release the blessings that come when the Ammonite curse is broken. Those blessings are compensation for the pains in my life that came from your hand. Do a supernatural work in me and in my world to position me to possess my birthright.

There is nothing too hard for you. There is no area of brokenness that you cannot redeem. I wait in expectation for you to work in me, through me, and around me, so that I can possess my birthright and so that the rivers of living water will flow from me to the world around me. Sever every tie to every unclean thing in the present or the past that would hold me back from experiencing your best. Fill every place that the enemy has vacated. Seal the work that has been done in me. Enforce every righteous decree. You are my King, and I have your protection because you love me, not because I deserve it. I proclaim your love, I celebrate your love, and I desire to live in your love. I ask these things in the mighty name of Jesus Christ, amen.

127

Blessing Of John

In the blessing of John, a person experiences fulfillment which comes from using all their abilities to do the task that God called them to do in partnership with his love and his power. Jephthah sought power and influence in a way he was not designed to have. John the Apostle was fascinated with power and authority while he was a young disciple (Luke 9:54; Mark 3:17). By the end of his life, he had lots of power and authority. He was the dominant apostle in the region of Asia Minor, pastoring in Ephesus. His impact was felt over the whole Christian movement for two centuries after his death. His high authority rivaled that of Paul in the depth and breadth of his influence in shaping Christianity. In addition to raising the dead, it is said that he was once thrown into a pot of boiling oil, but that could not kill him. Since he was un-killable, he was exiled to the island of Patmos. In spite of his achieving power and authority, it is clear in his writings that he recognized the greatest gift God had given him was a love relationship with Jesus. He was able to recognize the finest gift offered and not be dazzled by power and authority. Since he recognized it, he was able to receive it.

John was in the Spirit on the Lord's Day while on Patmos. Circumstances didn't matter. In the place of exile, he was still in love with the Lord and was enjoying that love relationship. He therefore possessed his birthright and was trusted by God with the most complex, wonderful, and comprehensive revelation of the nature of God recorded by anyone in history. Revelation is the culmination of the written Word. Few people recognize and receive the finest gifts God wants to give them. This is a great tragedy.

Signs Of The Blessing Of John

- Fulfillment is to accomplish the work your Father has given you. You do this by knowing who you are, being that person, and living a very fulfilling life doing your life's work every day.

- You enjoy every day synchronizing with God to fulfill your mission in the marketplace and the world. Because you lead with your large spirit, you get opportunities to represent Christ in secular settings.

- You know you are leaving a legacy that outlasts your life.

How To Develop In The Blessing Of John

- Make a list of the areas of your life where you received injustice but you lived in righteousness. Thank God for allowing those unjust circumstances. God chose to take everything away from Job who was righteous. God chose to give him the injustice so that he could give Job a double portion. Worship God as the God of the "some time later."

- Choose to live through injustice without being bitter. Live in expectation of God's compensation. God is not unjust in the fullness of time, although he may appear unjust for a moment in time.

Sevens In Scripture

Creation

The gift of mercy parallels the seventh day of creation (Genesis 2:2-3). On the first six days God was busy "doing." On the seventh day God was just "being." While the mercy is capable of doing many things, the mercy's heart is to enjoy God and be in his presence. God spent the seventh day savoring what he had done. Mercy moves at a slower speed because God designed them to extract the deepest amount of insight, understanding, and wisdom from what they experience. Mercy sees God's fingerprints in a more complex way than the other gifts. Knowledge of God comes to the mercy through the art of savoring him that no amount of analytical study will ever produce. God created nothing new on the seventh day, but he celebrated everything that he had created. Mercy celebrates what is good, right, and true. They have great alertness to and awareness of how the parts relate to the whole. They recognize alignment when all the pieces are in their right place. They are more sensitive than the other gifts to things not being in right alignment. Mercy has a craving for the ultimate alignment that God experienced on the seventh day of creation. Mercy draws from all the other gifts and in turn enhances all the other gifts. Mercy is the crown jewel of God's creation. God blessed the seventh day and sanctified it. The call of mercy is to celebrate God through worship and to sanctify time in their own lives and the lives of others.

Items Of Furniture In The Tabernacle

The seventh item of furniture is the mercy seat that was placed over the ark of the covenant (Exodus 25:17-22; 37:6-9). Mercy is given a wonderful promise, "There I will meet with you, and I will speak with you from above the mercy seat." The mercy seat was where the visible glory of God dwelled between the two golden cherubim. The mercy seat provided a way for the presence of God to dwell with his imperfect and unholy people without consuming them. The gift of mercy can transition from the unclean fallen world to the throne room with the greatest ease. Mercy is able to live in both worlds. God's call on the mercy gift is to erase the line between secular and sacred by bringing the fullness of God to all types of situations and people. This is the blessing of presence, where someone changes the spiritual climate around them simply by being there, without having to say or do anything. The gift of mercy has the ability to change the climate because they carry so much of the presence of God.

Compound Names of Jehovah

The seventh of the compound names of Jehovah is Jehovah-Shammah, "The LORD who is present" (Ezekiel 48:35). In Ezekiel 47-48 God gives instructions on how to divide the land for an inheritance among the twelve tribes of Israel. It concludes by saying "The distance around will be 18,000 cubits. And the name of the city from that time on will be The LORD is there." Most people with the gift of mercy desire and seek the presence of God for themselves. God's design for the mercy is to bring God's presence to their cities and regions, to bring the manifest presence of God to earth.

Seven Last Sayings On The Cross

Each one of the seven sayings of Jesus on the cross parallels a challenge for that redemptive gift. The seventh thing that Christ said on the cross was "Father, into your hands I commit my spirit." It seems like a simple task, but it represents one of the greatest challenges of the mercy gift. Jesus had cried out, "My God, my God, why have you forsaken me?" Now he was choosing to give his spirit to the same Father he accused of forsaking him. The gift of mercy has a simple solution for dealing with those who hurt them. They stay away from them. Christ had just been wounded very deeply by his Father who had abandoned him. But based on what was right, not what felt right, he committed his spirit into the hands of the very one who had caused him such pain. Ironically, mercy has few enemies yet seems in many ways to have some of the weakest reconciliation skills. When the mercy has been deeply wounded, often their default position is to walk away, raise a wall, maybe maintain contact with the person but never let them in. They stubbornly renounce any possibility of intimacy with the person who has wounded them. The mercy needs to leverage their great strength, which is intimacy with God, into a model of reconciliation. God is calling the mercy to do what Jesus did on the cross, to move toward the person who does not deserve it and offer them intimacy out of the overflow of their intimacy with God. The mercy also needs to take the initiative toward God in those times when the Father himself has hurt the mercy, when he goes through the desert and feels the silence of God. When the mercy has done everything he knows to do to be conformed to the will of God, and it seems that God is not moving and is ignoring him, he must choose to move toward God, rather than pulling back.

Seven Letters To The Churches In Revelation

The redemptive gift of mercy parallels the church of Laodicea in Revelation 3:14-22. *"You are wretched, poor, pitiful, blind, and naked. I counsel you to buy from me gold refined in the fire, so you can become rich; and white clothes to wear to cover your shameful nakedness; and salve to put on your eyes to see."* The gold refined in the fire refers to character. Revelation 19 shows that white clothes represent the good deeds of the saints. Eye salve is seeing in the spiritual realm the things that are more important than the natural realm. Mercy can mistakenly go after the comfort in the natural, being neither hot nor cold, accommodating people, but God says mercy is made for excellence in character, which is not developed in times of ease but in times of hardship. The gold refined in the fire is character that is the product of endurance, hard work, and diligence, systematically building the character of Christ. Mercy is called to have exquisite character that has been tried in the fire and proved to be worthy. God designed the mercy to pursue excellence, to have great character, to do a wealth of good deeds, and to see the treasures in the spiritual realm that God wants to show them. As they do these things, God will take great pleasure. In Laodicea he wanted to spit the believers out, but he said, "I am standing at the door knocking, asking to come in." The Father desires for the mercy to move toward Christ in an imperfect state and allow intimacy with him to produce the fruit of character and discernment. God does not need them to pull themselves up by their bootstraps to be pleasing to him. He delights to have intimacy which produces transformation.

"To him who overcomes, I will give the right to sit with me on my throne, just as I overcame and sat down with my Father on his throne. He who has an ear, let him hear what the Spirit says to the churches." Sitting on the throne can represents many things. It represents royalty, majesty, beauty, being set apart or above commoners. The mercy's design is to crave the intimacy that comes from being a co-regent with Jesus Christ and the satisfaction in their spirit that comes from being surrounded with the ultimate beauty and perfection of the throne room. God designed the mercy gift with a desire for excellence, visual excellence, excellence in presentation, and desire for inclusion and connectedness in intimacy with God. The mercy will never achieve the beauty of the throne and the throne room of heaven in this life, but it is the call of the mercy gift to try to find alignment, to bring beauty, to bring expression here on earth of what they will experience in heaven. The mercy should create their best masterpiece here on earth, bringing some of heaven to earth, while continuing to yearn for the things to come.

Blessing Prayer For Mercy

I bless you and honor you for your special place as the most complex and most sensitive of the gifts. You are the crown jewel of God's creation. The apostle John is the model for your gift, with his intimate and confidential relationship with Jesus.

I bless you for your safety for those who are wounded. You tend to attract people who are having mental and emotional distress. I bless your initiative toward wounded ones. You know who is feeling rejected, excluded or wounded. People, even strangers, can safely share their pain. You can touch a grieving heart with your quick release of tears.

I bless your deep power of compassion, the most healing of all human emotions. A biblical model for what mercy does is the Good Samaritan, who was sensitive and responsive to the needs of the wounded man when other travelers passed by on the other side. He identified with the man who fell among thieves. He had courage to translate caring into practical action. He did what he did because he was the man that he was.

I bless your loyalty to those you love. You are quick to take up the offenses of family and friends when they are rejected or mistreated. You draw away from those who are insensitive to others.

I bless your ability to sense genuine love. You have a large number of acquaintances and people who enjoy you, but you may have only a few close intimate friends. I bless your need for deep friendships in which there is mutual commitment and closeness. You have great expectations from friendships and can be deeply hurt by disappointments in friends. Jesus is your only Friend who will never disappoint.

I bless the totally different language that you speak, the language of the heart that is sometimes too deep for logic or for words. I bless you as you try to speak the language that your spirit does not have vocabulary for. I bless how you can recognize and capture God's presence in the ordinary events of everyday life. You see the beauty in the smallest things. You take time to smell the roses and appreciate unplanned moments of goodness. You communicate so much with your eyes, your touch, and your attention. You are frustrated when others don't understand this. You don't like people to try to re-engineer you into being something you are not.

I bless your desire for closeness. You measure acceptance by physical closeness and quality time together. You crave intimacy of soul, physical touch, hugs, communication, and contact. God designed you for intimacy in body, soul, and spirit. He will make a way for its holy and righteous expression by his grace.

I bless you with God's perspective on pain. Without his perspective, you can see no spiritual benefit to pain and suffering. When you avoid pain, the discipline of God may be wasted, because he builds righteousness and maturity through the discipline of pain. You may react to God's purposes in allowing people to suffer, and you want to remove the cause of pain quickly. I bless you to keep your eye on the joy set before you: to share in his holiness, a harvest of righteousness and peace for those who are trained by discipline, by pain, by struggle.

132

I bless you to turn to God for comfort when you are hurting. You can be sensitive, easily injured by the words and actions of others. You have a hard time healing from injury and processing and expressing what you are feeling. Others say to you, "Just get over it." This lack of understanding can cause you to withdraw and shut down. I bless you to pursue God of all comfort and Father of mercies, who will move into the pain and minister life where healing is needed.

I bless you with healthy, God-ordained boundaries. You can become a burden-bearer for burdens God does not intend you to bear, if you absorb pain from people who want to dump their pain on you. You don't have to absorb everybody's burdens. Jesus daily bears your burdens. His yoke is easy, and his burden is light (Matthew 11:29-30). Trust him to help you process emotions. I bless you to breathe deeper, live more freely, and connect more with people and God as you refuse to carry unholy burdens.

I bless your decision-making processes. You tend to be slow to make transitions based on emotional processing. It's not wrong; it's uniquely you. You do not like change; you require longer to disengage emotionally and re-engage in the next thing. I bless you as you let God take you through this process in his time.

I bless your ability to experience life differently. God wired you to operate intuitively. You feel the heart of God and make significant decisions based on your heart. That is your God-given appropriate language. I bless you for connecting with your heart and putting the other gifts in touch with processing that is spirit to spirit. You hear from God but have difficulty explaining the "why." The first six gifts typically hear God with their mind in a linear, logical way, but you hear and understand God with your spirit before your mind can explain what your spirit heard. I bless you to be free to say, "I don't know how I know. I just know. I don't have words."

I bless you to represent God in tough love. You hate to confront anybody. You may find it hard to be firm and decisive because you don't want to offend. You tend to avoid decisions and firmness until not deciding will cause greater hurt. When you are operating below the maximum of your gifting, you may bless what is broken or even sinful. An enabler will sympathize with those who violate God's standards to preserve the feelings of others. I bless your design by God to be absorbed in his holiness so that there is no way to enable brokenness or sinfulness.

You do not like to take sides or choose between two people. You may be seen as indecisive, because you do not want to hurt anybody or say they are wrong. Your highest authority will come when you are so aligned with God's perspective that you can appeal to those in sin and encourage them to come into alignment with God. Your model is Jesus who only did what he saw his Father doing. I bless you as you embrace your responsibility to see that which is clean and complete and aligned with God and bless others to raise the standard.

I bless you to let Father God re-father you and show you who you really are. Let him heal your wounds of earthly fathering and authorities. I bless you to let your heavenly Father establish you in your spirit. I bless you to be deeply fathered by him, until there is no fear, insecurity, or roots of rejection or abandonment, so that you have freedom, wholeness, willingness to risk,

133

inclusion, and belongingness. I bless you to step into your proper place in your heavenly Father, so you can live out your birthright.

Your spirit is not meant to be passive or to allow injustice. I bless you to win the battle against the victim mindset that attracts infirmity, financial devouring, physical abuse, sexual assault, or dishonor. You are a covenant child of the Most High God. You have dignity, honor, authority, and a special place in God's dominion. I bless you to rise up and live in all that you are in God.

You dislike and avoid warfare until you are pushed into a corner. When you see the pain others suffer, you can be drawn into spiritual warfare as a last resort. You are intended to master the art of worship as warfare. I bless you as you lift up the glory of God, his power, his miracles and his works, his names, reminding all of heaven, earth and hell that we serve God Most High. That is a radical disruption of the powers of evil around you.

I bless your creativity that raises the water table of the spiritual life of your faith community. You are drawn to the arts that allow you to express your love of God or vent the pain you feel or say visually what you do not have words for. Your sensitive spirit can express prayer, praise, reflection, peace, forgiveness, or reconciliation and connect them with the five senses. You appreciate creative expression and beauty in the spiritual life of the church.

Your spirit knows you are made to worship. You seek the face of God in intimacy. You are called to fulfillment by connecting with the Spirit of God and easily going into his presence to absorb his holiness and glory and bring others there. You can release the holiness of the glory of God into the world, and I bless you as you impart the blessing of presence and alignment to people, land, the environment, and buildings. I bless you to absorb the holiness of God in the holy of holies, and then release the blessing of his holiness and to align that which is crooked or warped.

On the seventh day God aligned, sanctified, and celebrated everything he had already made. You celebrate the rightness of everything God has done and is doing. You know what right alignment is when all the pieces are in their right place. You are alert to how the parts relate to the whole. You are right to feel in your spirit that there is something more. I bless your innate knowing that there is another dimension of beauty, excellence, and perfection where everything is so right it resonates in heavenly keys and rhythms. I bless you with moving toward alignment in the spirit realm where the spirit brings out the best of the soul, and the spirit and the soul are releasing the finest of what the body can do. That is your birthright.

I bless you with becoming the guardian of God's alignment with your blessing of presence. I bless you as God releases you into the fullness of who you were made to be — knowing your Father, blessing others, and releasing holiness to their sprits. You are called to be large-spirited. I bless you with authority and dominion in the community of the spirit. I bless you in the name of the 7-fold Spirit of the true and living God, amen.

The Bigger Picture

Redemptive Gifts Grid I

Gift	Principle vs. Battlefield	Authority	Birthright	Major Weaknesses
Prophet	**Design** vs. Fractured relationships	Principles for speaking life, light, and truth that call forth destiny	To help others live in their destiny by providing vision on God's design	Non-relational Judgmental Bitterness and unforgiveness
Servant	**Authority** vs. Mindset of victimization	Pray for leaders, restore families, love the hard cases	To be a life-giver to others, especially leaders. To provide the cleansing and authority others require for their destiny	Battle for self-worth Worry/anxiety Enabling
Teacher	**Responsibility** vs. Selective responsibility	Generational blessing as they bring forth fruit	To know God's deep truths and to know him experientially. To reveal the presence of God to others	Passive Selective responsibility Sight vs. faith Doctrine vs. intimacy
Exhorter	**Sowing And Reaping** vs. Denial	Influence through relationships. Reconciliation to God and others	To reveal God to others. To mobilize large numbers of people to act on God's will	People-pleasing Poor time management Compromise
Giver	**Stewardship** vs. Ownership and independence	To detect, bring forth, protect, and nurture new birth	To release life-giving generational blessings into the family line. To produce life-giving systems through holiness and intimacy with God	Independence Hypocrisy Manipulation and control
Ruler	**Freedom** vs. Exploitation	Highest level of generational blessings that bring freedom	To release spiritual generational blessings physically and spiritually by honoring God's agenda	Insensitivity Ethics/integrity Substituting his agenda for God's agenda
Mercy	**Fulfillment** vs. Futility	Intimacy with God and alignment	To release the holiness of God into their environment. To come into the presence of God and worship God in all of life	Impurity Mixture of holy and unholy Enabling to protect from pain

135

Redemptive Gifts Grid II

Gift	Foundational Principles	Demonic Strongholds	Root Iniquity	Essential Virtues	Curses On The Birthright	Causes Of The Curse	Blessings Needed For Effectiveness
Prophet	Purpose, design, and truth	Fractured relationships	The rights of Individuals	Being a rebuilder	**Aramean** Can't get justice	Adultery or molestation in the family line	**Hosea** Favor
Servant	Authority	Victim Spirit	Peace at any cost	Walking in dominion	**Moabite** No platform for success	Poverty spirit, fear of loss, inability to grasp identity	**Esther** Secure borders, resources for life
Teacher	Responsibility	Religious spirit	Selective responsibility	Sanctifying his family	**Philistine** Lacks key resources, one piece missing blocks project	Using religiosity to legitimize wrong behavior	**Daniel** Supernatural strategies, receiving from God
Exhorter	Sowing and reaping	The cult of comfort	Denial	Embracing the pain	**Canaanite** Oppressive work load	Denial and entitlement. Using influence to persuade others to do wrong	**Moses** Time to develop finest abilities
Giver	Stewardship	Ownership	Control	Walking by faith	**Midianite** Seasonal devouring of money & family relationships	Putting personal comfort ahead of responsibility to nurture family	**Job** Accruing capital
Ruler	Freedom	Predator Spirit	Exploitation	Being life-giving	**Jotham's** Betrayal from within	Covenant-breaking. Lawlessness	**Nehemiah** Life-giving community and institutions
Mercy	Fulfillment	Self-gratification	Stubbornness	Pleasing God, not man	**Ammonite** Barrenness	Inability or failure to accept God's view & his love of you.	**John** God helping you possess your birthright

Seven In Scripture

Gifts	Days Of Creation	Furniture In The Tabernacle	Compound Names Of God	Churches In Revelation	Last Sayings Of Christ On The Cross
Prophet	Light	Brazen altar	Jehovah-Jireh God Provides	Ephesus	Father, forgive them, for they do not know what they are doing
Servant	Atmosphere	Bronze laver	Jehovah-Rophe God heals	Smyrna	I tell you the truth, today you will be with me in paradise
Teacher	Dry Land	Table of showbread	Jehovah-Nissi God is my banner	Pergamum	Dear woman, here is your son; here is your mother.
Exhorter	Sun, moon, and stars	Golden lamp stand	Jehovah-Shalom God is my peace	Thyatira	My God, my God why have you forsaken me?
Giver	Life in sea and air	Altar of incense	Jehovah-Rohi God is my shepherd	Sardis	I am thirsty
Ruler	Land animals and humans	Ark of the covenant	Jehovah-Tsidkenu God is my righteousness	Philadelphia	It is finished
Mercy	Rest	Mercy seat	Jehovah-Shammah God is there	Laodicea	Father, into your hands I commit my spirit

The Redemptive Gifts In Real Life

If all seven of the redemptive gifts visited a person who is sick in the hospital, they would say...

What principle do we learn from this? What is God trying to say to you through this illness?

Prophet

I brought your mail in, fed your dog, watered your plants, and washed your dishes, and here is a little gift that you will need while you are sick.

Servant

Teacher

I've done some research on your illness, and I can explain what is happening.

How do you feel? I can't begin to tell you how bad I felt when I heard you were sick.

Mercy

Don't worry about a thing. I've assigned your job to four other people in the office.

Ruler

Exhorter

I just stopped by to check in on you and see how you are doing.

Giver

I thought I'd come by and cheer you up. Have you had many visitors? I met a real nice lady down the hall...

Note: Givers typically would not stay long. They would have a quick exit strategy if they did not sense a "real value" in staying longer.

If a child spilled his milk at the dinner table, and if each of the seven gifts were represented in a family, they would say...

That's what happens when you are not careful.

Prophet

Motivation: to fix the problem by pointing out the "why"

I'll clean it up.

Servant

Motivation: to fulfill a practical need

The reason the glass tipped over was that it was put in the wrong place.

Teacher

Motivation: to explain what happened

Well, as they say, it's not worth crying over, so have I told you the one about the cow who ...

Exhorter

Motivation: to minimize the interruption and get back to the fun environment, being sensitive to the child's emotional state

No problem. It happens. Let's clean it up and keep on going.

Giver

Motivation: to restore peace and move forward, to show the child how to handle it in the future

Jim, get a towel. Sue, pick up the glass. Mary, pour another glass of milk.

Ruler

Motivation: to respond to the problem to achieve the immediate goal of the group to have a nice meal together

Don't feel bad. It could happen to anyone. I spilled my milk once, too.

Mercy

Motivation: to relieve embarrassment and to empathize with the discomfort

139

How Do The Redemptive Gifts Go On Vacation?

Prophet

Ideal Spot: Wide open spaces and very few people. A prophet on vacation wants to sit on the rim of the Grand Canyon, just him and God, without having to talk with the locals. The prophet wants to discover new history and new concepts, not build relationships. He dislikes group tours and cruises with no purpose.

Servant

Ideal Spot: Anywhere as long as he can do something to serve. When going to the beach, he makes sure everybody has an umbrella and suntan lotion and they can eat and drink what they want for lunch. Would prefer going on a work project or missions trip, rather than to an all-inclusive spa where others are constantly serving him.

Teacher

Ideal Spot: Somewhere he has not been before. The teacher does not go the same place twice (unless he didn't see everything the first time). The teacher enjoys thoroughly researching every logistic. Teachers will know what the location is known for and which restaurants are rated the highest. He will methodically go through the museums, reading every sign and leaving no stone unturned. He makes sure it's done correctly and doesn't like the pressure of balancing everybody's desires. He leaves the vacation looking toward the next place to research and learn about.

Exhorter

Ideal Spot: A cruise or resort location where there is a party all the time with lots of people to interact with and a variety of fun things to do, and no responsibility. He likes to have something that is larger than life to talk about when he gets home.

Giver

Ideal Spot: One of two locations. 1. A place where he can be spontaneous, no reservations, just get in the car and see where it takes him. Givers don't like vacation plans that lock them into "have to be here or there" situations. He wants the flexibility to stay another day, if desired. 2. A vacation with a purpose, maybe traveling to another location and teaching a seminar while he is there. Givers tend not to like vacations just for the sake of doing nothing. He needs to see the value in going on the vacation.

Ruler

Ideal Spot: A vacation that he can organize or administer. He likes organizing a family reunion, camping trip, or a ski trip for a group where there is work to be done and jobs to delegate to others. Rulers thrive under pressure with a group to administer. He likes the pressure of the new project and seeing a plan come together. It is very difficult for rulers to just sit still. He will find a project to work on, if there is not one presented to him.

Mercy

Ideal Spot: A place where he can do nothing, relax, and just "be." The mercy doesn't like to vacation alone. He prefers to go with others, but he wants lots of options for activities so that everyone's needs are met. He struggles with making choices between two options, because he doesn't want to hurt somebody's feelings. If someone else expresses a strong opinion, he will go along with them, rather than stand up for his own agenda.

Redemptive Gifts Of Cities And Nations

Cities and nations have been established by God's hand, not by accident, pressures of sociological occurrence, or migrations of people. God commanded Adam and Eve to be fruitful and multiply. God desires the earth to be inhabited. He determines the times when nations are born and die. God determines the place where nations and cities live (Acts 17:26). Over half of Scripture is written to nations and communities. God is passionate about communities and people groups (Revelation 5:9; 7:9).

The term "spiritual mapping" was born out of a need for new understanding of strongholds operating in our cities and nations. It became evident that there are both past iniquities and blessings laid up in the history of our cities. Regardless of what iniquity has occurred in a city or nation, God was there first. He formed the earth and everything in it. Redemptive gifts are resident in both the people and the land. The corporate gifting is resident in the land. Within a community, there are catalytic people or groups which are instrumental in bringing into being the redemptive gifts of these places. The ultimate goal of the study of redemptive gifts of cities is to draw people to God. God does not want any to perish. The redemptive gifts are tools in God's toolbox so that all may know Jesus Christ as Savior.

Definitions of Terms

Behavioral characteristics: outward defining social behavior of a city or nation that reflects a redemptive gift.

Stronghold: a mindset that causes you to accept something that is contrary to the will of God.

Birthright: one thing that is unique to a city that no other city has.

Redemptive gift released: when every institution in the city is life-giving and it has possessed its birthright for itself and for other cities around it.

The research for information on the United States is primarily from Microsoft Encarta Encyclopedia. Some sentences were lifted verbatim, and this note is to credit this source for the information provided. I also wish to recognize this as a good source for historical research.

Redemptive Gift Of Prophet In A City Or Nation

Behavioral Characteristics Of The City Or Nation

- Resistance to bondage or being told what to do — desire to be free.

- Bitterness — elections highly contested, ancient disputes (i.e., South Carolina and Civil War).

- Extreme discrimination, yet has a heart for the poor.

- Drive for excellence, does things better (architecture, infrastructure, etc.).

- Profound ability to communicate.

- Ideological seedbed, innovative ideas, trail-blazing.

- Profound despair when hope is taken away.

- Quick to take initiative in conflict.

Stronghold Of The City Or Nation

Fragmentation of relationships.

Root Iniquity

Acceptance and normalization of bitterness.

Virtues To Foster For Effective Authority In Intercession

- Invest in relationships, both new and broken, at personal expense.

- Cultivate relationship with God first and foremost — dependence on God, faith in him alone.

- Be intentional about spiritual fathering, nurturing, and discipling the next generation.

Signs Of A City Or Nation Walking In Its Redemptive Gift

- Becomes a community of racial unity and family restoration.

- New ideas released for taking cities: spiritual technological center, theological excellence.

- Becomes a champion of spiritual freedoms with a warfare anointing.

- Spiritual fathering occurs and the younger generation is blessed.

We will look at several examples of states whose redemptive gifts have been identified. Understand that this is not a perfect science and that there are disagreements among those who have studied redemptive gifts of states. Focus on the methodology used, and you will better understand the identification process. An additional list of cities, states, and nations is also included at the end of each redemptive gift section.

Examples Of US States With Gift Of Prophet

South Carolina

The root of rebellion can be traced back to at least the 1680's when colonists tried to overthrow the proprietors of the colony so as to come under the control of the royal government of England. Subsequent history shows them nursing grievances endlessly and turning to force frequently. They are an ideologically driven people, and this is God's design. Heretofore, satan has used their gift to keep them looking at the problems around them as well as things in the past. This inward, backward focus can keep the state from being used for the greatest good. South Carolina was designed by God to be a catalytic state. When it can see the grandeur of the future from God's perspective, it will be able to galvanize the east coast into repudiating the cult of comfort and fighting for the spiritual freedom that is the birthright of the nation.

Massachusetts

The Edomite curse runs deep. On one hand, Massachusetts violently opposes any loss of freedom, real or perceived. On the other hand, it has historically oppressed religious and racial minorities. Its schools of higher education and its high tech industries are outlets for the prophet's passion to be on the cutting edge. Would to God that this passion for excellence and being on the cutting edge was manifested in and through the Body of Christ. Cotton Mather well said, "Religion hath begat prosperity, and the daughter hath devoured the mother."

West Virginia

While this state officially separated from Virginia during the Civil War, the roots of the division were ancient. Typical of a ruler society, Virginia's land aristocracy blatantly discriminated against the small farmers of the remote part of the state. Typical of a prophet society, the West Virginians resented anything that resembled injustice or control. The state sent thousands into both armies during the Civil War, leaving deep wounds in the spirit of families within the state. Subsequent labor and political battles have been deep, bitter, violent and wounding. The state was made to die for ideology. When it is able to commit to seeing the kingdom of light and life triumph over the kingdom of darkness and death, it will have an influence vastly greater than its size. It has a long tradition of guerilla warfare and could easily provide some of the most skilled, creative, and intrepid warriors the church has ever seen.

Other Cities, States, And Nations With Gift Of Prophet

Cities: Atlanta, GA; Boston, MA; Delano, CA; Fillmore, CA; Linwood, CA; Oildale, CA; Signal Hill, CA. **States:** Texas. **Countries:** Afghanistan, Apache Indian Nation, Eritrea, Germany, Hungary, Scotland, Spain, Syria, United States.

Redemptive Gift Of Servant In A City Or Nation

Behavioral Characteristics Of The City Or Nation

- Mantle of dishonor and invisibility for community — endless jokes, no fame, unwanted land, treated below the reality of who they are.

- High amount of agricultural and service industries.

- Exploitive leadership.

- Attracts predators and victims — domination instead of dominion. High levels of abuse, domestic violence, child molestation.

- Government leadership problem — lack of and need for strong elected leaders.

- Not offensive or disruptive, blends into the background. Often overlooked.

Stronghold Of The City Or Nation

Mindset of victimization.

Root Iniquity

Denying one's God-given identity.

Virtues To Foster For Effective Authority In Intercession

- Become a life-giver to others. Speak the truth to liberate.

- Walk in dominion: nurturing, shepherding, and empowering. Be proactive.

- Focus prayer toward leaders, defiled land, death, and other areas of need.

Signs Of A City Or Nation Walking In Its Redemptive Gift

- Healing of the family unit.

- Ecological restoration.

- Tenacity in delivering the gospel and heart for evangelism.

- Highest authority given because they don't want it.

- Authority for cleansing land, heavenlies, and leadership.

- Authority of community affects worldwide moves of the Spirit.

Examples Of US States With Gift Of Servant

Georgia

James Oglethorpe and his partners planned the colony as a refuge for the poor, especially those in debtors' prisons. He hoped to create a model society where none would be rich or poor. Those sent to Georgia at the trustee's expense received 50 acres of land and supplies to get them started. No family was allowed to sell, lease, or even will the land away. Strong drink and slavery were prohibited. The idealistic beginning was eventually negated by the power of greed and oppression. The removal of the Cherokee Indians to Oklahoma and Sherman's march to the sea are only two of many cases of severe exploitation of the people. That history notwithstanding, the spiritual foundation of the colony had much in it that was excellent. When Boston breaks the Edomite Curse over the nation, and the prototype of racial healing is established in Philadelphia, that prototype can be implemented on a grand scale in Georgia. There has been a massive move of African Americans back to Georgia from the north in the last 50 years as God has set the stage for healing. Atlanta has the gift of prophet with a strong predatory drive. Savannah is teacher gift with the first Masonic temple in America and the first Jewish synagogue.

Delaware

Delaware was always the victim of other nations' wars. Control of the area passed from the Dutch to the Swedes to the Dutch to the English to the Dutch to the English. Under the English, the territory was variously claimed by William Penn, Lord Calvert, and the local residents who didn't really want to be part of either adjacent colony. Delaware has served industry well. First, there was the duPont family and subsequently the banking and credit card industries. With the wave of corporate mergers, Delaware changed its laws to facilitate incorporation in the state and minimize the takeovers. In the natural, it serves to protect the business interests of the nation. In the spiritual, it could empower new ministries to the business community. As God pours out his Spirit in commerce, this would be an ideal state for protecting and nurturing this new move of God so that it grows to become international in scope.

Other Cities, States, And Nations With Gift Of Servant

Cities: Almalonga, Guatemala; Bethlehem, Israel; Bakersfield, CA; Garden Grove, CA; Marengo Valley, CA; Mohave, CA. **States**: New Mexico, Nevada. **Countries:** El Salvador, India, Portugal, Sudan, Suriname, Vietnam, Zambia.

Redemptive Gift Of Teacher In A City Or Nation

Behavioral Characteristics Of The City Or Nation

- Number of hospitals, research facilities, and educational institutions is disproportionately high to the population.

- High number of restaurants with fine cuisine and ethnic cuisine.

- Tendencies toward geographic and social divisions, usually a geographic divide such as a river, mountain, or valley.

- Religious spirit — feeling of having an inside line on the truth, turf wars, a large number of churches, many birthed out of church splits.

- Focus on the past — proud of heritage, museums.

- Defilement of land and buildings, overt Satanism, Freemasonry presence and dedication.

- Many parks and cemeteries.

- City of refuge for those who want to rest or escape, a harbor of hospitality.

- Passivity in all sectors of society — leaders make soft choices for convenience or control.

- Transportation system with arteries going out, many highways, railroads, or river.

- Passive military presence.

Stronghold Of The City Or Nation
False worship.

Root Iniquity
Selective responsibility.

Virtues To Foster For Effective Authority In Intercession

- True Spirit-filled worship of God as a lifestyle, not just worship services.

- Recognize God's fingerprints in everyday life.

- Build responsibility. Maintain a high level of integrity in practical ways: pick up litter, return phone calls, place shopping cart in cart return, etc.

Signs Of A City Or Nation Walking In Its Redemptive Gift

- Evidence of presence of God manifested publicly.

- Known as a city of refuge, place of healing, restoration to wholeness.

- Justice, biblical truth, and righteousness all in proper alignment.

- Serves as a prototype to other city and nations.

- Generational anointing.

- Authority in intercession to redeem ministries that fall short of fulfilling their godly purpose.

Examples Of US States With Gift Of Teacher

New Jersey

New Jersey has the highest concentration of colleges and universities as well as the largest pharmaceutical industry in the nation. Its call is to bring forth healing truth that can be used by the surrounding states.

North Carolina

This gift brings an anointing for developing prototypes of new ideas. This is illustrated by the Wright brothers traveling from Ohio to North Carolina in order to test their airplane. The Research Triangle Park, with apexes focused on the University of North Carolina at Chapel Hill, Duke University in Durham, and North Carolina State University in Raleigh, shows us in the natural what the spiritual heritage of the state is. There should be a constant flood of new spiritual wisdom and strategy coming from this state. It also has a vibrant Native American community numbering over 70,000 from nine nations. These bear witness to the fact that the state is a safe place for the wounded to heal. Franklin Graham's Samaritan's Purse is a high profile example of a healing ministry, but there are many other less known places of refuge and restoration provided by the Body of Christ in the state.

Pennsylvania

The state was populated by religious refugees from England and Germany who brought with them a significant victim spirit. The birthright of the state is to be a major influence in national affairs. From the inception of William Penn's involvement, he pushed local representation and a grass roots involvement in civil affairs. However, because of the past woundedness, there was tension from the beginning with citizens focusing on real and imaginary wrongs, rather than looking at their personal responsibility. Over the years, the state has attracted many predatory businesses, and the victims have responded wrongly with violence. This in turn has resulted in violence from business and government to suppress the violence from the victims. Some of the bloodiest defeats in America's various wars were suffered in Pennsylvania. The state still has the calling to turn the course of the nation, but it must throw off the victim spirit and walk in the dominion God has called it to. No one can do this for them. It must reject the lie and own the truth. Then life will flow to it as it flows through it to the nation.

Other Cities, States, And Nations With Gift Of Teacher

Cities: Baltimore, MD; Berlin, Germany; Birmingham, AL; Budapest, Hungary; Colorado Springs, CO; Jerusalem, Israel; Katmandu, Nepal; Kansas City, KS/MO; Long Beach, CA; Nashville, TN; Oakhurst, CA; Pasadena, CA; Philadelphia, PA; San Antonio, TX; Savannah, GA; Silver City, NM; Slidell, LA; Tampa Bay, FL; Waco, TX; Yucca Valley, CA. **Countries:** Barbados, Kurdistan, Tibet.

Redemptive Gift Of Exhorter In A City Or Nation

Behavioral Characteristics Of The City Or Nation

- Has a high profile.

- Normalization of sin and iniquity.

- Seedbed of successful evangelism.

- Relationships are strong. Makes room for different people groups without conflict.

- Relationships valued above doctrine.

- Major economic component is trade/commerce, especially retail, etc.

- Susceptible to godless spirit.

- Entertainment is paramount. Large presence of entertainment industry. Focus is on self.

Stronghold Of The City Or Nation

Self-centeredness, comfort focus.

Root Iniquity

Refusal to confront sin if it would jeopardize relationship.

Virtues To Foster For Effective Authority In Intercession

- Walk in reality. Call sin what it is, seek the glory of God, seek holiness.

- Intentional focus on relationships: willingness to experience rejection, stress, and discomfort.

- Having high moral standards and no compromise.

Signs Of A City Or Nation Walking In Its Redemptive Gift

- Influence over many people for kingdom purposes.

- Reconciliation with power.

- God's message to the world comes forth.

- Fingerprints of God on the city.

- Purity vs. compromise, move toward purity in the church.

- Supernatural vs. natural, embracing the holy supernatural.

Examples Of US States With Gift Of Exhorter

Vermont

Vermont was first in abolition and in giving universal suffrage to all males, regardless of race or land ownership. When the Anti-Masons ran a candidate for president, he carried this state. The Anti-Masonic party dominated the state legislature in the early 1800s. There was significant lawlessness in the business community as they smuggled goods into and out of Canada during times of war. They quietly looked to their own interests, regardless of what the national policies were.

California

The geographic territories with the gift of exhorter have had a significant impact in world history. California has an empire-building, expansionist component to their DNA. It is not low profile in any dimension. Los Angeles is a major worldwide communication and broadcasting center for all fields of entertainment. God designed it to be a communications center for his glory to the world. But the exhorter gift has been severely perverted in world history, causing as much damage as it has good. The normalization of sin, particularly sensuality, in entertainment stands out. California has the reputation for its entitlement mindset and anything goes. Entertainment and the focus on self may begin with acceptable soul pleasure, but too often it descends into overt sensuality. Think of the R-rated movies and pornography that come out of California. The city of Los Angeles produces about 80% of the world's pornography, especially child pornography, and justifies it. The attitude is "This is the way the culture is, it's a non-issue."

Fads and trends frequently start in California. Silicon Valley gave birth to the popular computer industry and caused it to flourish, and with the exhorter's propensity for bigger and better, it spread around the world. California has a major financial component. If it were a country, at one time it would have the fifth largest gross national product in the world. California has a huge amount of diversity, particularly diversity of cultures. It can receive conflicting groups of people, make room for them, and keep them from amalgamating. There can be diversity without tension, conflict, or hostilities. There is centralized government with a high degree of control from the state level. In California, many businesses left the state and went elsewhere, because the state business laws have become more and more complex and more and more detailed, creating more and more of a burden.

Other Cities, States, And Nations With Gift Of Exhorter

Cities: Amsterdam, Netherlands; Chicago, IL; Lakewood, CA; Los Angeles, CA; Paris, France; Santa Clarita, CA. **Countries:** Argentina, France, Italy, Mexico, Roman Empire, Wales.

Redemptive Gift Of Giver In A City Or Nation

Behavioral Characteristics Of The City Or Nation

- Intense diversity on every front — race, economy, denominations, restaurants.

- Generational birthing anointing for industries, ministries, etc., when operating righteously but can be known to squelch the birthing of new ideas and ministries.

- Independent spirit (negative and positive). Known for busyness.

- Religious spirit. Event-focused rather than relationship-focused.

- Provides vital resources, serves as a resourcer.

- High focus on safety. Excellent fire and police services.

- Not ordinarily aggressive in warfare. Looks for a way around it, reactive.

- Complex politics, often corrupt.

- High profile entertainment.

- Known as a catalyst for networking, with international implications and connections.

Stronghold Of The City Or Nation

Control through spirits of Leviathan and Jezebel. Leviathan is empowered through pride in competence. Jezebel is empowered through wrong response to pain.

Root Iniquity

Fear that kills faith.

Virtues To Foster For Effective Authority In Intercession

- Depend on God. Be willing to risk vulnerability to allow God to supply needs.

- Be a life-giver to others.

- Pray that people walk in vulnerability to break the independent spirit.

- Bless and do not curse.

- Celebrate little things in a day. Diversity in celebration. Gratefulness disempowers Leviathan.

Signs Of A City Or Nation Walking In Its Redemptive Gift

- Birthing anointing to give the world a faith-based model.

- Lies, deception, and control of Freemasonry and religious spirit are broken.

- Heart of God revealed through evangelism.

- Faith and thankfulness are present.

Examples Of US States With Gift Of Giver

Maine

There is a significant victim spirit. It was not until just before the Civil War that Maine was even acknowledged as a separate state. Massachusetts kept Maine under its thumb. Presently about five lumber companies own half of the state.

Rhode Island

This state has huge internal contradictions. It has the strongest religious freedom record, as well as the ugliest anti-immigrant record. It was one of the main slave trading states, yet it emancipated slaves in 1808. The chief cities in the state were founded by religious leaders, yet because of the spirit of rebellion of those dissidents, lawlessness in government and business has been epidemic. It has a good record of dealings with the Native Americas. There is an anointing for life springing up from that which appears to be dead. The Narragansett Indians were declared extinct in 1880, but they regrouped and received tribal lands again in 1978.

New York

This state experiences ideological confusion as the giver takes a short-term pragmatic approach to life. It has a record of exploiting workers, yet it is the birthplace of much social reform and employment benefits. Historically, there has always been massive corruption in government, yet there is strong support for law-and-order candidates. It resists strong central government, yet embraces strong individual leaders. One quarter of the Jews in America live in New York State. It was the birthplace of Susan B. Anthony and Elizabeth Cody Stanton, who pushed women's rights. It was also the birthplace of the Mormons and the Anti-Masonic political party.

Florida

Florida is in a battle to determine whether the state will minister to the soul of a person or the spirit. For decades it has been a major tourist/retirement area that promises a multitude of pleasures for the soul. However, in the last 30 years some major men of God have come from Florida and touched the world. Now there is an emerging pattern of international ministries, such as Campus Crusade for Christ and Wycliffe Bible Translators, moving their headquarters to Florida. The state was designed by God to provide the platform from which anointed worship, intercession, and evangelism could flood the world, not just the nation. The tension between the soul and the spirit is present but still low key. Eventually, there will be a moment of decision as the church in the state has to decide whether to pay the price to possess their birthright. It is like Jacob and Esau, both seeing the promise but having different values. Pray that the Body of Christ in this state will not sell their birthright for a mess of potage.

Other Cities, States, And Nations With Gift Of Giver

Cities: Boynet Park, CA; Chattanooga, TN; Dallas, TX; Hilton Head, SC; New York, NY; North Pole, AK; Plato, MO; San Jose, CA. **States:** Kentucky, Louisiana. **Countries:** Armenia, Brazil, Cuba, Israel, Japan, Kenya, Philippines, Netherlands, Nigeria, South Africa, South Korea, Switzerland.

Designed For Fulfillment

Redemptive Gift Of Ruler In A City Or Nation

Behavioral Characteristics Of The City Or Nation

- Obsession with expanding its borders, will battle to do so. Major expansionist component, aggressive annexation.

- Known for endurance and resurgence.

- Exploitation of the masses by the ruling class (predator spirit) for gain.

- Very politically adept. Can get done what it wants done.

- Healthy independence, busy, vibrant, energetic. Doesn't need world opinion, sees no need to justify actions. Doesn't look back.

- Empire-building. Constant appetite for bigger borders.

- High number of gated communities.

- Existence of central government. May be the county seat.

- Governing by control in the church, focus on organization building, mega-churches.

Stronghold Of The City Or Nation
Predator.

Root Iniquity
Exploiting people for the sake of the project (especially economic projects).

Virtues To Foster For Effective Authority In Intercession

- Leadership is to nurture, shepherd, and empower.

- Serving is the key. Reject the need to control others.

- Church must serve the community.

- Victims have the authority to bless or curse.

- Walk in daily dependence on God, not on the arm of the flesh.

Signs Of A City Or Nation Walking In Its Redemptive Gift

- Crime rates down, families remain together, business flourishes, God's purposes shown in government.

- Generational blessing released through leaders.

- Releases blessing over nations for following God's natural laws.

- Nations are drawn to it because they are looking for a good model to rule with.

- Becomes a place where the impossible happens.

152

Examples Of US States With Gift Of Ruler

Connecticut

This state claims to have the first written constitution. It leads in wartime, not just with people but with the military technology to support a war effort. There is a command-and-control mentality throughout the state that produces the usual predator/victim spirit problem. It is the richest state in per capita wealth, yet their three primary cities—Bridgeport, Hartford and New Haven—are among the poorest in the nation. The anointing for business expansion is so great that General Electric and Union Carbide moved their headquarters to the state. Connecticut also hosts the corporate offices of many major insurance companies. Hartford has the gift of giving. Financial institutions, insurance, and real estate account for one third of the state's gross product. It dominates the nation's printing, publishing, and cultural life.

Virginia

This state combined effectively with the prophet state of Massachusetts to drive the Revolutionary War and with the prophet state of South Carolina to drive the Civil War. Historically, the state has provided a disproportionate number of political and military leaders to the nation. The Pentagon and a critical Marine base are in Virginia. This birthright for providing national leaders has surfaced in the church in Pat Robertson's ministry, as well as Jerry Falwell's work. This, however, is just a taste of what the state could provide to the nation, should the Body of Christ in the state step into the fullness of their inheritance.

Other Cities, States, And Nations With Gift Of Ruler

Cities: Fresno, CA; Santa Anna, CA; Ventura, CA; Washington, DC. **State:** Mississippi.
Countries: China, Egypt, England, Ethiopia, Russia.

Redemptive Gift Of Mercy In A City Or Nation

Behavioral Characteristics Of The City Or Nation
- Intolerance of intolerance.
- Tolerance of diversity of different views, worship, cults, Eastern mysticism, etc.
- City of refuge. Example, San Francisco is a refuge for the gay community.
- Tolerance of immorality and sexual sin. Anything goes. Example, New Orleans.
- Creativity and self-expression.

Stronghold Of The City Or Nation
False fulfillment of body, soul, and spirit.

Root Iniquity
Pride in denial.

Virtues To Foster For Effective Authority In Intercession
- Fulfillment within God's boundaries in the body: seek pleasure in godly relationships.
- Fulfillment within God's boundaries in the soul: celebrate soulish things blessed by God.
- Fulfillment within God's boundaries in the spirit: find fulfillment in the presence of God.
- Restore people intentionally. Rebuild lives.

Signs Of A City Or Nation Walking In Its Redemptive Gift
- A place of high worship with an open heaven. God's manifest presence in and over the community.
- No line or separation between the secular and sacred.
- Enjoyment of life as an act of worship.
- Acceptance of broken, rejected people with the power of God to heal and restore.
- Bodies liberated, healed, set free into the presence of God.
- Wisdom of God is evident.
- Becomes a city of influence.
- Release of all these things to the nations.

Examples Of US States With Gift Of Mercy

Maryland

The colony was birthed as a place of refuge for oppressed Catholics, and they firmly extended religious protection to Protestants as well. The state three times voted down referenda designed to disenfranchise black voters. Thurgood Marshall, a Baltimore attorney, won the landmark civil rights case *Brown v. Board of Education* that required the desegregation of schools. He later became the first black justice on the Supreme Court. As with any other mercy community, there was a historic resistance to proud outsiders telling them what to do. The gift of teacher does its best work when it is in partnership with the gift of mercy. Thus, God put Jerusalem (teacher) in the tribe of Benjamin (mercy) and Baltimore (teacher) in Maryland (mercy) so as to bring those two cities to their highest potential.

New Hampshire

New Hampshire has a remarkable lack of victim spirit. There is a high adaptability to change. They are prone to neutrality, but when the nation goes solidly in one direction, they will follow. They have gone to amazing lengths to keep from taxing people. They tax the land and the businesses. They have a state legislature of 400 people in an attempt to keep any group of people from feeling excluded from the legislative process.

Other Cities, States, And Nations With Gift Of Mercy

Cities: New Orleans, LA; Paia, Maui; San Francisco, CA; Whittier, CA. **State:** Hawaii.
Countries: Canada, Norway.

Where Do You Go From Here?

Understanding your design and developing the potential God placed in you is a lifelong journey. The ultimate purpose of this study is to assist each person to discover the masterpiece that he is. As each of you discover who you really are and begin to walk in your birthright, the Father is glorified, you and those around you are transformed, and the world is impacted. As you continue your journey in developing your gift, I encourage you to keep pursuing the following things.

Embrace Your True Identity In Christ

God made you to be who you are and to do what he made you to do. Begin to do things in your gifting, and discover how God wants to use you and your gift. Don't let fear of failure or fear of rejection stop you from discovering who God created you to be. Everyone has characteristics and tendencies that we don't like. It is human nature to look around at other people, see their gifts, and want their particular gift, but that is rejection of self and of God's design. There is no "higher high" than to be living and functioning in who God created you to be and to be doing exactly what he created you to do.

Become More Like Christ

Every gift has a battlefield of Christ-likeness he must win in order to possess his birthright. Gifts are given. Fruit is grown. To live out of your gift to the maximum and possess your birthright, become more like Christ in those areas that are battlefields for you. Be intentional about working on, developing, and maturing in character, values, and discipline. There is a price to pay to live in your gifting. God is more interested in your character than your gifts. Pay the price to grow in these areas so that you will display the fullness of God's design.

Realize How Much You Need Others With Their God-Given Gifts

The gifts are not for your honor or your power. They help you serve and bless others and glorify Christ. Don't deny others the gifts and talents that God has given you. You will be blessed as you bless others. The gifts and passions that God gave you can come together in unexpected ways to serve the body. Remember that the purpose of the gifts is to reveal Jesus. The purpose of Jesus is to reveal the Father. The gifts weave a beautiful tapestry of sons and daughters of the Most High. With all the gifts woven together, we see more of God as we are his presence-bearers.

Learning From The Other Gifts

A prophet may speak the truth but not in love, as Jesus commanded us to do. So a prophet can learn love from the gift of mercy. The exhorter needs to learn from the teacher about spiritual accuracy and validation of truth. The teacher needs to learn from the exhorter how to make the truth practical in everyday terms. God's design is a win-win proposition. His design is for the body of Christ to experience the greatest benefit at the same time that we experience our greatest joy. We experience fulfillment, we experience joy, we possess our birthright, we live in our identity, and the body of Christ is expanded. That is what the redemptive gifts are all about.

157

Designed For Fulfillment

Epilogue

The study of the redemptive gifts is a work in progress. **_Designed For Fulfillment_** is merely an introduction to a vast subject. There is more for each of us to discover as we continue to learn new facets of the gifts. We challenge you to own this material. Be a learner in this new field of exploration. Personally add to, subtract from, and clarify the material as you go. There are several blank pages throughout the book so that you can write your own notes, insights, and personal applications. Add to, subtract from, and clarify the material periodically as needed. We are all learning, and adapting, and growing, and perhaps what we believe today will have to be refined in the future. Even if you do not pursue going deeper, we are confident that you will find this material alone is a tremendous asset to your understanding of redemptive gifts.

Your constructive thoughts are invited. Feel free to share any insights that you receive as you use this material. You may have another piece to the puzzle that we need to see. We would also love to hear how God uses his truth in your life.

Arthur Burk has stated many times that a father is not a father until someone they father, fathers another. If this is true, and I believe it is, then both you and I are not only called to be a son, but also a father. Arthur, Nina, and Sylvia were "sons" long before they became "fathers" to me. They took the truths in this book and helped me to better understand fathering and sonship. I am now carrying that torch and hope to leave a legacy of "fathering" others. I now challenge you to be a father too. You have been given life to be a life-giver. You have been blessed to be a blessing.

Index To Some Of Arthur Burk's Resources
From Plumbline Ministries and Amethyst Healing Concepts

This study of redemptive gifts is just the beginning. There is much more material available. Here are recommend resources to further your study and understanding of the redemptive gifts.

Prophet

CD Set Redemptive Gift Of Individuals, CD 2
CD Set The Seven Principles, CD 2 and 3
CD Set Seven Curses, CD 1*
CD Set Developing The Human Spirit

Servant

CD Set Redemptive Gift Of Individuals, CD 3
CD Set The Seven Principles, CD 4
CD Set Seven Curses, CD 2*
CD Set Developing The Human Spirit
Overcoming The Victim Spirit - free download (Library, Spiritual Warfare section)
Theft Of Honor - free download or CD
Praying For Leaders

Teacher

CD Set Redemptive Gift Of Individuals, CD 4
CD Set The Seven Principles, CD 5
CD Set Seven Curses, CD 3*
CD Set Developing The Human Spirit

Exhorter

CD Set Redemptive Gift Of Individuals, CD 5
CD Set The Seven Principles, CD 6
CD Set Seven Curses, CD 4*
CD Set Developing The Human Spirit

Giver

CD Set Redemptive Gift Of Individuals, CD 6
CD Set The Seven Principles, CD 7
CD Set Seven Curses, CD 5*
CD Set Developing The Human Spirit

Ruler

CD Set Redemptive Gift Of Individuals, CD 7
CD Set The Seven Principles, CD 8
CD Set Seven Curses, CD 6*
CD Set Developing The Human Spirit

Mercy

CD Set Redemptive Gift Of Individuals, CD 8
CD Set The Seven Principles, CD 9 and 10
CD Set Seven Curses, CD 7*
CD Set Developing The Human Spirit

*Renunciations for all of the curses are on CD 8

From Plumbline Ministries Web Library

Redemptive Gifts Grid With Principles
Summary Of Legitimacy Curses
Sevens In Scripture
The Seven Blessings
The Redemptive Gifts Of East Coast States
The Redemptive Gifts Of Some American States
The Redemptive Gifts Of Some Nations

General Resources

CD Set Redemptive Gifts Of Cities
CD Prophet And Giver
CD New Spiritual Authority: Intimacy
CD Set Ministering To Babies In The Womb (Some CDs Sold Separately)
CD Set Walking In Sonship
CD Set Spiritual Warfare
Book *Blessing Your Spirit*
Book *Relentless Generational Blessings*
Book *Pure Joy*

To Order From Arthur Burk

www.plumblineministries.com and **www.amethysthealingconcepts.com**
Or call Monday to Friday 8:30 am to 4:30 pm, Pacific time.
US: 888-635-6011 | International: 714-224-0126

Plumbline Ministries and Amethyst Healing Concepts are divisions of Sapphire Leadership Group
2367 West La Palma Avenue, Anaheim, CA 92801

To contact or order *Designed For Fulfillment*
Free To Be Ministries, Inc.
P. O. Box 1340, Amite, LA 70422

Website: www.freetobeministries.com
Email: chuck@freetobeministries.com
Phone: 601-749-8220
